WITH WORKBOOK

TOP NOTCH

English for Today's World

2A

WITH WORKBOOK

TOP NOTCH

English for Today's World

2A

Joan Saslow ■ Allen Ascher

With *Top Notch Pop Songs and Karaoke*
by Rob Morsberger

PEARSON
Longman

Top Notch: English for Today's World   2A with Workbook

Pearson Education, 10 Bank Street, White Plains, NY 10606

Editorial director: Pamela Fishman
Senior development editors: Martin Yu, Trish Lattanzio
Development editor: Geraldine Geniusas
Associate development editors: Siobhan Sullivan, Judy Li
Vice president, director of design and production: Rhea Banker
Director of electronic production: Aliza Greenblatt
Managing editor: Mike Kemper
Production editor: Michael Mone
Art director: Ann France
Senior manufacturing buyer: Dave Dickey
Photo research: Aerin Csigay
Digital layout specialist: Warren Fischbach
Text composition: Kirchoff-Wohlberg, Word & Image Design Studio, Inc.
Text font: Palatino 11/13, Frutiger 10/12
Cover photograph: "From Above," by Rhea Banker. Copyright © 2005 Rhea Banker.

Photo credits: All original photography by David Mager. Page 2 (top left) Will & Deni McIntyre/Getty Images, (top middle left) Michael Goldman/Masterfile, (top middle right) Robert Frerck/Odyssey Productions, Inc., (right) Jeff Greenberg/PhotoEdit, (left middle) Michael Newman/PhotoEdit, (Left middle left) Mark Hamilton/Dorling Kindersley; p. 3 David R. Frazier Photolibrary, Inc.; p. 5 (background) Luis Villota/Corbis, (left) Gary Conner/PhotoEdit, (top middle) Adam Woolfitt/Corbis, (bottom middle) David Sacks/Getty Images, (top right) Michal Heron, (bottom right) Bob Krist/eStock Photo; p. 6 (inset) Mathias Oppersdorff/Photo Researchers, Inc., (feijoada) Mourad Tarek/Stockfood America; p. 7 (left to right) Dallas & John Heaton/Corbis, Dallas & John Heaton/Corbis, John Neubauer/PhotoEdit, Renee Comet Photography/Stockfood America, Picture Finders Ltd./eStock Photo; p. 8 (middle) Gary Hunger/Getty Images; p. 11 (snake) Jerry Young/Dorling Kindersley, (octopus) Frank Greenaway/Dorling Kindersley, (pig) Mike Dunning/Dorling Kindersley, (cheese) Spencer Jones/Corbis, (Moscow) Jose Fuste Raga/eStock Photo, (Shanghai) Steve Vidler/eStock Photo, (Istanbul) John Henley/Corbis, (Honolulu) Vladpans/eStock Photo, (gliding) Sunstar/Photo Researchers, Inc., (sailing) Image du Sud/eStock Photo, (riding) Fritz Prenzel/Peter Arnold, Inc., (snorkeling) Norbert Wu/Peter Arnold, Inc.; p. 12 (upper top) Nik Wheeler/Corbis, (lower top) Gunter Marx Photography/Corbis, (bottom left to right) Renee Comet Photography/Stockfood America, SuperStock, Steve Vidler/eStock Photo, Tibor Bognar, Rafael Macia/Photo Researchers; p. 14 (background) Tom Daly/Getty Images, (top right) Photofest, (left) John Springer/Corbis, (bottom right) Royalty-Free/Corbis; p. 15 (middle) www.comstock.com; p. 16 (bottom) Dave Parker/Alpha/Globe Photos; p. 17 (background) Graham Monro/Photolibrary.com, (bottom) Shaun Egan/Getty Images; p. 18 (action) Original Films/Bob Marshak/The Kobal Collection, (comedy) Morgan Creek/The Kobal Collection, (documentary) AP Wide World Photos, (drama) Paramount/The Kobal Collection, (horror) Warner Bros/The Kobal Collection, (musical) 20th Century Fox/The Kobal Collection, (sci-fi) MGM/The Kobal Collection, (animated) Globe Photos (bottom) Clive Streeter/Dorling Kindersley; p. 22 (left) Warner 7 Arts/The Kobal Collection, (right) Bettmann/Corbis; p. 23 Rob Melnychuk/Getty Images; p. 30 (background) Ron Brown/SuperStock, (single) Jeff Greenberg/PhotoEdit, (double) Jeff Greenberg/PhotoEdit; p. 32 (background) Andrew McKim/Masterfile, (towels) www.comstock.com, (hangers) Jose Luis Pelaez, Inc./Corbis, (iron) Michael Matisse/Getty Images, (dryer) Getty Images, (make up) Jeff Greenberg/Index Stock Imagery, (turn down) www.comstock.com, (bring up) David Bartruff Inc.; p. 33 Andy Crawford/Dorling Kindersley; p. 34 (left) Dorling Kindersley, (middle) Rudi Von Briel/PhotoEdit, (right) Bernard Boutrit/Woodfin Camp Associates; p. 38 (computer) Stockbyte, (bottom) Steve Gorton/Dorling Kindersley; p. 44 (background) Photolibrary.com, (sedan) Courtesy DaimlerChrysler Corporation, (wagon) Tim Ridley/Dorling Kindersley, (convertible) David Young-Wolff/PhotoEdit, (luxury) Ron Kimball Photography, (SUV) Kurt Wittman/Corbis, (van) David Young-Wolff/PhotoEdit, (compact) Greg Martin/SuperStock, (full) Ron Kimball/Ron Kimball Stock, (sports) Adam Woolfitt/Corbis; p. 46 (top right) Corbis Digital Stock, (left) Spike/Getty Images; p. 51 Getty Images; p. 56 (inset left) Jose Luis Pelaez/Corbis, (inset right) Billy Hustace/Getty Images; 57 (right) Dorling Kindersley, (bottom) Barnabas Kindersley/Dorling Kindersley; p. 58 (top) Michael Bermant, MD, Board Certified, American Board of Plastic Surgery, www.plasticsurgery4u.com, (bottom) Yoav Levy/Phototake; p. 59 Bill Losh/Getty Images; p. W1 (1) Will & Deni McIntyre/Getty Images, (2) Michael Goldman/Masterfile, (3) Robert Frerck/Odyssey Productions, Inc., (4) Jeff Greenberg/PhotoEdit; p. W4 Angelo Cavalli/Index Stock Imagery; p. W17 Reuters/Corbis; p. W20 Dan Gair/Index Stock Imagery; p. W25 (top) Kevin Fleming/Corbis, (middle) Wendell Metzen/Index Stock Imagery, (bottom) Royalty-Free/Corbis; p. W27 Fredde Lieberman; p. W30 Lawrence Manning/Corbis; p. W44 Steve Dunwell Photography, Inc./Index Stock Imagery; p. W47 The New Yorker Collection 1992 J.B. Handelsman from cartoonbank.com All rights reserved; p. W53 Getty Images.

Illustration credits: Steve Attoe, pp. 6, 24, W5, W24, W39 (top); Sue Carlson, p. 35; John Ceballos, pp. 10, 25, 37, 49, 61; Mark Collins, pp. 27, 42; Leanne Franson, pp. W6, W32 (top), W43; John Hovell, pp. 9, 46; Brian Hughes, pp. 15, 22, 40, 41, 42, 47, 55, W29 (bottom), W31; Stephen Hutchings, p. W21, Suzanne Mogensen, pp. W23, W39 (bottom); Andy Myer, p. 17; Dusan Petricic, pp. 8, 33, 41, W9, W27, W37; Jake Rickwood, p. 20; Neil Stewart, pp. 50, W45; Anne Veltfort, pp. 31, 54; Jean Wisenbaugh, p. 13.

ISBNs: 0-13-110491-8 (Student's Book with Workbook and Audio CD)
    0-13-238703-4 (Student's Book with Workbook and Take-Home Super CD-ROM)

Printed in the United States of America
4 5 6 7 8 9 10–QWD–10 09 08 07

Contents

REFERENCE SECTION FOR 2A AND 2B

WORKBOOK

Scope and Sequence FOR 2A AND 2B

UNIT	Vocabulary*	Conversation Strategies	Grammar	
1 **Greetings and Small Talk** *Page 2* *Top Notch* Song: "Greetings and Small Talk"	• Customs around the world • Tourist activities	• Ask <u>What have you been up to?</u> or <u>How have you been?</u> to start a conversation • Add information beyond <u>Yes</u> or <u>No</u> to continue a conversation • Use <u>That's great</u> to shift to a new topic	• The present perfect: <u>yet</u>, <u>already</u>, <u>ever</u>, and <u>before</u> • past participles	• Further explanation of form and usage: the present perfect
2 **Movies and Entertainment** *Page 14* *Top Notch* Song: "Better Late Than Never"	• Explanations for being late • Ways to express likes and dislikes • Movie genres • Adjectives to describe movies	• Use <u>They say</u> to support a suggestion • Use <u>Actually</u> to indicate that what you are about to say may be surprising • Use <u>For real?</u> to convey surprise	• The present perfect: additional uses—<u>for</u> and <u>since</u> • <u>Would rather</u>	• Contrasting the present perfect and the present perfect continuous • Spelling rules for the present participle
3 **Staying at Hotels** *Page 26*	• Telephone messages • Hotel room features • Hotel facilities • Hotel room amenities and services	• Use <u>I'd like to</u> to politely state your purpose on the phone • Use <u>That's right</u> to confirm • Use <u>By the way</u> to introduce a new topic or a question	• The future with <u>will</u> • <u>Had better</u>	• Further explanation of usage: future with <u>will</u> and <u>be going to</u> • Degrees of obligation: <u>have to</u>, <u>must</u>, <u>had better</u>, <u>be supposed to</u>, <u>should</u>, <u>ought to</u>, and <u>could</u>
4 **Cars and Driving** *Page 38* *Top Notch* Song: "Wheels around the World"	• Ways to show concern • Car parts • Types of cars • Bad driving behaviors • Polite address • Phrasal verbs	• Use expressions such as <u>I'm so sorry</u> and <u>How awful</u> to convey concern • Begin a response with <u>Well</u> to introduce an explanation	• The past continuous • Direct object placement with phrasal verbs	• Further explanation of usage: the past continuous • Direct object placement: separable and inseparable phrasal verbs
5 **Personal Care and Appearance** *Page 50*	• Personal care products • Salon services • Ways to schedule and pay for personal care • Ways to improve appearance	• Repeat part of a question before answering to clarify • Use <u>Can I get</u> to make a request more polite	• Count and non-count nouns: indefinite quantities and amounts—<u>some</u>, <u>any</u>, <u>a lot of</u>, <u>many</u>, and <u>much</u> • <u>Someone</u> and <u>anyone</u>	• Review of non-count nouns: containers, quantifiers, and other modifiers • <u>Too many</u>, <u>too much</u>, and <u>enough</u> • Indefinite pronouns: <u>something</u>, <u>anything</u>, and <u>nothing</u>

*In *Top Notch*, the term *vocabulary* refers to individual words, phrases, and expressions.

Speaking	Pronunciation	Listening	Reading	Writing
• Offer to introduce someone • Get reacquainted with someone • Greet a visitor • Talk about tourist activities • Explain local customs • Ask about life experiences	• Negative contractions	• People ask visitors about what they've done <u>Task</u>: identify activities • A game show <u>Task</u>: describe the guests' life experiences • Conversation with a visitor <u>Task</u>: identify tourist sights visited	• Magazine article about gestures around the world • Customs around the world • Experiences survey	• Write about an experience • Create a guide for visitors to your country on how to behave • Introduce yourself
• Apologize for and explain lateness • Offer to pay or return the favor • Compare tastes in movies • Describe movies you've seen lately • Discuss the effects of violence in the media	• Reduction of /h/	• Movie reviews <u>Task</u>: identify genres and recommendations • Two people choose a movie to see <u>Task</u>: write movie descriptions • Conversations about movies <u>Task</u>: use adjectives to describe the movies	• Magazine article about violence in movies • Movie catalog ads • Movie reviews	• Write a movie review page • Express opinions about violence in media
• Leave and take a phone message • Check into and out of a hotel • Discuss hotel room features and facilities • Request housekeeping services • Choose a hotel	• Contractions with <u>will</u>	• Phone calls to a hotel <u>Task</u>: take phone messages • Conversations about hotel reservations <u>Task</u>: write the room features guests want • Requests for hotel room amenities and services <u>Task</u>: identify the services and items requested	• Tourist guide recommending New York hotels • Hotel bill • Hotel preference survey	• Describe the advantages and disadvantages of a hotel • Describe a hotel you've stayed at
• Describe a car accident and damage • Express concern • Ask for service and repairs • Describe car problems • Rent a car • Discuss driving rules	• Stress of particles in phrasal verbs	• People describe car accidents <u>Task</u>: identify car damage • Phone calls to a car rental agency <u>Task</u>: infer if the caller rented the car • Conversations with a car rental agent <u>Task</u>: listen for car types	• Magazine article about driving abroad • Online response to car rental request • International road signs • Driving safety survey	• Compare good and bad drivers
• Shop for personal care products • Ask for something you can't find • Request salon services • Schedule and pay for personal care • Discuss ways people improve their appearance	• Vowel reduction to /ə/	• Radio advertisements <u>Task</u>: identify personal care products • Conversations about salon appointments <u>Task</u>: identify salon services • Customers ask about personal care services <u>Task</u>: listen for the services requested and explain what happened	• Advice column about cosmetic surgery • Personal appearance survey	• Write a letter to a magazine's editor • Describe a personal care product you like

Scope and Sequence FOR 2A AND 2B

GRAMMAR BOOSTER

UNIT	Vocabulary	Conversation Strategies	Grammar	
6 **Eating Well** *Page 62*	• Excuses for not eating something • Food passions • Lifestyles and health problems • Describing food	• Use <u>Don't worry about it</u> to decline an apology • Use <u>Well</u> to introduce an opinion that differs from someone else's	• Negative <u>yes</u> / <u>no</u> questions and <u>Why don't</u> …? • <u>Used to</u>	• Further explanation of usage: negative <u>yes</u> / <u>no</u> questions with short answers • Further explanation of usage: <u>Why don't / doesn't</u> …? • Further explanation of form: <u>used to</u>
7 **Psychology and Personality** *Page 74* *Top Notch* Song: "The Colors of Love"	• Describing colors • Adjectives of emotion • Suggestions to cheer someone up • Adjectives to describe personality	• Use <u>You know,</u>... to be less abrupt • Use <u>out of the question</u> to indicate opposition • Use <u>Really?</u> to indicate a difference of opinion • Use <u>Thanks for asking</u> to acknowledge another's concern	• Gerunds and infinitives after certain verbs • Gerunds after prepositions • Expressions with prepositions	• Further explanation of form and usage: gerunds and infinitives • Negative gerunds
8 **Enjoying the Arts** *Page 86* *Top Notch* Song: "To Each His Own"	• Types of art • Common materials • Positive adjectives • Ways to say you don't like something	• Use <u>For one thing</u> to provide one reason among several • Use <u>Excuse me</u> to ask for attention in a store	• The passive voice: statements and questions	• Further explanation of form and usage: the passive voice • The passive voice: intransitive verbs
9 **Living with Computers** *Page 98*	• Computer products and accessories • Computer toolbars and commands • Internet activities	• Use <u>Oh yeah?</u> to show that you are interested • Use <u>Everyone says</u> to solicit an opinion • Use <u>Well</u> to soften a contradictory opinion • Use <u>Why don't you</u> to respectfully offer advice	• Comparisons with <u>as</u> … <u>as</u> • The infinitive of purpose	• Review: comparatives and superlatives • <u>As</u> … <u>as</u> with adverbs • Expressing purpose with <u>in order to</u> and <u>for</u>
10 **Ethics and Values** *Page 110*	• Ways to acknowledge thanks • Ways to express certainty • Moral dilemmas • Personal values	• Use <u>Excuse me</u> to get a stranger's attention • Ask <u>You think so?</u> to probe the wisdom of a course of action	• Possessive pronouns • Factual and unreal conditional sentences	• Further explanation of form and usage: factual and unreal conditional sentences

Speaking	Pronunciation	Listening	Reading	Writing
• Offer dishes and decline food • Talk about foods you love and hate • Discuss lifestyle changes • Describe unique foods	• Used to	• Conversations about food Task: identify excuses for not eating something • Descriptions of food passions Task: determine each person's food passions • Descriptions of unique foods Task: describe food items	• News article about changing lifestyles and obesity • The healthy-eating pyramid • Lifestyle survey	• Write about lifestyle changes • Describe a dish
• State color preferences • Describe your mood and emotions • Cheer someone up • Discuss personatlity types • Discuss the impact of birth order on relationships	• Reduction of to in infinitive phrases	• Conversations about color preferences Task: write color names and adjectives of emotion • An academic lecture Task: infer definitions of personality • Conversations about emotions Task: describe how each speaker feels about certain things	• Magazine article about the impact of birth order on personality • Color survey • Personality survey	• Describe your own personality • Describe the personality of someone you know well
• Recommend a museum • Describe an object • Describe how you decorate your home • Discuss your favorite artists • Express opinions about art	• Emphatic stress	• A biography of Vincent Van Gogh Task: listen for his life events • Conversations about art objects Task: identify the objects discussed	• Magazine article about the role of art in two people's lives • Guide to London museums	• Create a short biography of an artist you like • Describe a piece of art you like
• Discuss buying a computer product • Recommend "a better deal" • Troubleshoot a problem • Describe how you use computers • Discuss the benefits and problems of the Internet	• Stress in as … as phrases	• Conversations about using computers Task: identify computer commands • Descriptions of computer activities Task: listen for things to do on the Internet • Conversations comparing two computer products Task: complete comparative sentences	• Four news articles about serious problems with the Internet • Electronics store website • Consumer information card	• Express your opinion about the social impact of the Internet • Report how you use a computer
• Return lost property • Discuss an ethical choice • Express personal values • Discuss honesty • Warn about consequences	• Assimilation of the sounds /d/ + /y/	• Conversations about personal values Task: identify each person's personal values and infer meaning of key words and phrases	• News article about the Tokyo lost-and-found • Values self-test	• Express opinions about modesty • Write an article about appropriate appearance in your country • Narrate a true story about an ethical choice

Acknowledgments

Top Notch International Advisory Board

The authors gratefully acknowledge the substantive and formative contributions of the members of the International Advisory Board.

CHERYL BELL, Middlesex County College, Middlesex, New Jersey, USA • ELMA CABAHUG, City College of San Francisco, San Francisco, California, USA • JO CARAGATA, Mukogawa Women's University, Hyogo, Japan • ANN CARTIER, Palo Alto Adult School, Palo Alto, California, USA • TERRENCE FELLNER, Himeji Dokkyo University, Hyogo, Japan • JOHN FUJIMORI, Meiji Gakuin High School, Tokyo, Japan • ARETA ULHANA GALAT, Escola Superior de Estudos Empresariais e Informática, Curitiba, Brazil • DOREEN M. GAYLORD, Kanazawa Technical College, Ishikawa, Japan • EMILY GEHRMAN, Newton International College, Garden Grove, California, USA • ANN-MARIE HADZIMA, National Taiwan University, Taipei, Taiwan • KAREN KYONG-AI PARK, Seoul National University, Seoul, Korea • ANA PATRICIA MARTÍNEZ VITE DIP. R.S.A., Universidad del Valle de México, Mexico City, Mexico • MICHELLE ANN MERRITT, Proulex/Universidad de Guadalajara, Guadalajara, Mexico • ADRIANNE P. OCHOA, Georgia State University, Atlanta, Georgia, USA • LOUIS PARDILLO, Korea Herald English Institute, Seoul, Korea • THELMA PERES, Casa Thomas Jefferson, Brasilia, Brazil • DIANNE RUGGIERO, Broward Community College, Davie, Florida, USA • KEN SCHMIDT, Tohoku Fukushi University, Sendai, Japan • ALISA A. TAKEUCHI, Garden Grove Adult Education, Garden Grove, California, USA • JOSEPHINE TAYLOR, Centro Colombo Americano, Bogotá, Colombia • PATRICIA VECIÑO, Instituto Cultural Argentino Norteamericano, Buenos Aires, Argentina • FRANCES WESTBROOK, AUA Language Center, Bangkok, Thailand

Reviewers and Piloters

Many thanks also to the reviewers and piloters all over the world who reviewed *Top Notch* in its final form.

G. Julian Abaqueta, Huachiew Chalermprakiet University, Samutprakarn, Thailand • David Aline, Kanagawa University, Kanagawa, Japan • Marcia Alves, Centro Cultural Brasil Estados Unidos, Franca, Brazil • Yousef Al-Yacoub, Qatar Petroleum, Doha, Qatar • Maristela Barbosa Silveira e Silva, Instituto Cultural Brasil-Estados Unidos, Manaus, Brazil • Beth Bartlett, Centro Colombo Americano, Cali, Colombia • Carla Battigelli, University of Zulia, Maracaibo, Venezuela • Claudia Bautista, C.B.C., Caracas, Venezuela • Rob Bell, Shumei Yachiyo High School, Chiba, Japan • Dr. Maher Ben Moussa, Sharjah University, Sharjah, United Arab Emirates • Elaine Cantor, Englewood Senior High School, Jacksonville, Florida, USA • María Aparecida Capellari, SENAC, São Paulo, Brazil • Eunice Carrillo Ramos, Colegio Durango, Naucalpan, Mexico • Janette Carvalhinho de Oliveira, Centro de Linguas (UFES), Vitória, Brazil • María Amelia Carvalho Fonseca, Centro Cultural Brasil-Estados Unidos, Belém, Brazil • Audy Castañeda, Instituto Pedagógico de Caracas, Caracas, Venezuela • Ching-Fen Chang, National Chiao Tung University, Hsinchu, Taiwan • Ying-Yu Chen, Chinese Culture University, Taipei, Taiwan • Joyce Chin, The Language Training and Testing Center, Taipei, Taiwan • Eun Cho, Pagoda Language School, Seoul, Korea • Hyungzung Cho, MBC Language Institute, Seoul, Korea • Dong Sua Choi, MBC Language Institute, Seoul, Korea • Jeong Mi Choi, Freelancer, Seoul, Korea • Peter Chun, Pagoda Language School, Seoul, Korea • Eduardo Corbo, Legacy ELT, Salto, Uruguay • Marie Cosgrove, Surugadai University, Saitama, Japan • María Antonieta Covarrubias Souza, Centro Escolar Akela, Mexico City, Mexico • Katy Cox, Casa Thomas Jefferson, Brasilia, Brazil • Michael Donovan, Gakushuin University, Tokyo, Japan • Stewart Dorward, Shumei Eiko High School, Saitama, Japan • Ney Eric Espina, Centro Venezolano Americano del Zulia, Maracaibo, Venezuela • Edith Espino, Centro Especializado de Lenguas - Universidad Tecnológica de Panamá, El Dorado, Panama • Allen P. Fermon, Instituto Brasil-Estados Unidos, Ceará, Brazil • Simão Ferreira Banha, Phil Young's English School, Curitiba, Brazil • María Elena Flores Lara, Colegio Mercedes, Mexico City, Mexico • Valesca Fróis Nassif, Associação Cultural Brasil-Estados Unidos, Salvador, Brazil • José Fuentes, Empire Language Consulting, Caracas, Venezuela • José Luis Guerrero, Colegio Cristóbal Colón, Mexico City, Mexico • Claudia Patricia Gutiérrez, Centro Colombo Americano, Cali, Colombia • Valerie Hansford, Asia University, Tokyo, Japan • Gene Hardstark, Dotkyo University, Saitama, Japan • Maiko Hata, Kansai University, Osaka, Japan • Susan Elizabeth Haydock Miranda de Araujo, Centro Cultural Brasil Estados Unidos, Belém, Brazil • Gabriela Herrera, Fundametal, Valencia, Venezuela • Sandy Ho, GEOS International, New York, New York, USA • Yuri Hosoda, Showa Women's University, Tokyo, Japan • Hsiao-I Hou, Shu-Te University, Kaohsiung County, Taiwan • Kuei-ping Hsu, National Tsing Hua University, Hsinchu, Taiwan • Chia-yu Huang, National Tsing Hua University, Hsinchu, Taiwan • Caroline C. Hwang, National Taipei University of Science and Technology, Taipei, Taiwan • Diana Jones, Angloamericano, Mexico City, Mexico • Eunjeong Kim, Freelancer, Seoul, Korea • Julian Charles King, Qatar Petroleum, Doha, Qatar • Bruce Lee, CIE: Foreign Language Institute, Seoul, Korea • Myunghee Lee, MBC Language Institute, Seoul, Korea • Naidnapa Leoprasertkul, Language Development Center, Mahasarakham University, Mahasarakham, Thailand • Eleanor S. Leu, Souchow University, Taipei, Taiwan • Eliza Liu, Chinese Culture University, Taipei, Taiwan • Carlos Lizárraga, Angloamericano, Mexico City, Mexico • Philippe Loussarevian, Keio University Shonan Fujisawa High School, Kanagawa, Japan • Jonathan Lynch, Azabu University, Tokyo, Japan • Thomas Mach, Konan University, Hyogo, Japan • Lilian Mandel Civatti, Associação Cultural Brasil-Estados Unidos, Salvador, Brazil • Hakan Mansuroglu, Zoni Language Center, West New York, New Jersey, USA • Martha McGaughey, Language Training Institute, Englewood Cliffs, New Jersey, USA • David Mendoza Plascencia, Instituto Internacional de Idiomas, Naucalpan, Mexico • Theresa Mezo, Interamerican University, Río Piedras, Puerto Rico • Luz Adriana Montenegro Silva, Colegio CAFAM, Bogotá, Colombia • Magali de Moraes Menti, Instituto Lingua, Porto Alegre, Brazil • Massoud Moslehpour, The Overseas Chinese Institute of Technology, Taichung, Taiwan • Jennifer Nam, IKE, Seoul, Korea • Marcos Norelle F. Victor, Instituto Brasil-Estados Unidos, Ceará, Brazil • Luz María Olvera, Instituto Juventud del Estado de México, Naucalpan, Mexico • Roxana Orrego Ramírez, Universidad Diego Portales, Santiago, Chile • Ming-Jong Pan, National Central University, Jhongli City, Taiwan • Sandy Park, Topia Language School, Seoul, Korea • Patrícia Elizabeth Peres Martins, Instituto Brasil-Estados Unidos, Rio de Janeiro, Brazil • Rodrigo Peza, Passport Language Centers, Bogotá, Colombia • William Porter, Osaka Institute of Technology, Osaka, Japan • Caleb Prichard, Kwansei Gakuin University, Hyogo, Japan • Mirna Quintero, Instituto Pedagógico de Caracas, Caracas, Venezuela • Roberto Rabbini, Seigakuin University, Saitama, Japan • Terri Rapoport, Berkeley College, White Plains, New York, USA • Yvette Rieser, Centro Electrónico de Idiomas, Maracaibo, Venezuela • Orlando Rodríguez, New English Teaching School, Paysandu, Uruguay • Mayra Rosario, Pontificia Universidad Católica Madre y Maestra, Santiago, Dominican Republic • Peter Scout, Sakura no Seibo Junior College, Fukushima, Japan • Jungyeon Shim, EG School, Seoul, Korea • Keum Ok Song, MBC Language Institute, Seoul, Korea • Assistant Professor Dr. Reongrudee Soonthornmanee, Chulalongkorn University Language Institute, Bangkok, Thailand • Claudia Stanisclause, The Language College, Maracay, Venezuela • Tom Suh, The Princeton Review, Seoul, Korea • Phiphawin Suphawat, KhonKaen University, KhonKaen, Thailand • Craig Sweet, Poole Gakuin Junior and Senior High Schools, Osaka, Japan • Yi-nien Josephine Twu, National Tsing Hua University, Hsinchu, Taiwan • Maria Christina Uchôa Close, Instituto Cultural Brasil-Estados Unidos, São José dos Campos, Brazil • Luz Vanegas Lopera, Lexicom The Place For Learning English, Medellín, Colombia • Julieta Vasconcelos García, Centro Escolar del Lago, A.C., Mexico City, Mexico • Carol Vaughan, Kanto Kokusai High School, Tokyo, Japan • Patricia Celia Veciño, Instituto Cultural Argentino Norteamericano, Buenos Aires, Argentina • Isabela Villas Boas, Casa Thomas Jefferson, Brasilia, Brazil • Iole Vitti, Peanuts English School, Poços de Caldas, Brazil • Gabi Witthaus, Qatar Petroleum, Doha, Qatar • Yi-Ling Wu, Shih Chien University, Taipei, Taiwan • Chad Wynne, Osaka Keizai University, Osaka, Japan • Belkis Yanes, Freelance Instructor, Caracas, Venezuela • I-Chieh Yang, Chung-kuo Institute of Technology, Taipei, Taiwan • Emil Ysona, Instituto Cultural Dominico-Americano, Santo Domingo, Dominican Republic • Chi-fang Yu, Soo Chow University, Taipei, Taiwan, • Shigeki Yusa, Sendai Shirayuri Women's College, Sendai, Japan

To the Teacher

What is *Top Notch*?

- *Top Notch* is a six-level communicative English course for adults and young adults, with two beginning entry levels.
- *Top Notch* prepares students to interact successfully and confidently with both native and non-native speakers of English.
- *Top Notch* demonstrably brings students to a "Top Notch" level of communicative competence.

Key Elements of the *Top Notch* Instructional Design

Concise two-page lessons

Each easy-to-teach two-page lesson is designed for one class session and begins with a clearly stated communication goal and ends with controlled or free communication practice. Each lesson provides vocabulary, grammar, and social language contextualized in all four skills, keeping the pace of a class session lively and varied.

Daily confirmation of progress

Adult and young adult students need to observe and confirm their own progress. In *Top Notch*, students conclude each class session with a controlled or free practice activity that demonstrates their ability to use new vocabulary, grammar, and social language. This motivates and keeps students eager to continue their study of English and builds their pride in being able to speak accurately, fluently, and authentically.

Real language

Carefully exposing students to authentic, natural English, both receptively and productively, is a necessary component of building understanding and expression. All conversation models feature the language people really use; nowhere to be found is "textbook English" written merely to exemplify grammar.

Practical content

In addition to classic topical vocabulary, grammar, and conversation, *Top Notch* includes systematic practice of highly practical language, such as: how to leave and take a phone message, how to request services at a hotel, how to make excuses to decline food you don't like, how to recommend a better deal—usable language today's students want and need.

Memorable model conversations

Effective language instruction must make language memorable. The full range of social and functional communicative needs is presented through practical model conversations that are intensively practiced and manipulated, first within a guided model and then in freer and more personalized formats.

High-impact vocabulary syllabus

In order to ensure students' solid acquisition of vocabulary essential for communication, *Top Notch* contains explicit presentation, practice, and systematic extended recycling of words, collocations, and expressions appropriate at each level of study. The extensive captioned illustrations, photos, definitions, examples, and contextualized sentences remove doubts about meaning and provide a permanent in-book reference for student test preparation. An added benefit is that teachers don't have to search for pictures to bring to class and don't have to resort to translating vocabulary into the students' native language.

Learner-supportive grammar

Grammar is approached explicitly and cognitively, through form, meaning, and use—both within the Student's Book units and in a bound-in Grammar Booster. Charts provide examples and paradigms enhanced by simple usage notes at students' level of comprehension. This takes the guesswork out of meaning, makes lesson preparation easier for teachers, and provides students with comprehensible charts for permanent reference and test preparation. All presentations of grammar are followed by exercises to ensure adequate practice.

English as an international language

Top Notch prepares students for interaction with both native and non-native speakers of English, both linguistically and culturally. English is treated as an international language, rather than the language of a particular country or region. In addition, *Top Notch* helps students develop a cultural fluency by creating an awareness of the varied rules across cultures for: politeness, greetings and introductions, appropriateness of dress in different settings, conversation do's and taboos, table manners, and other similar issues.

Two beginning-level texts

Beginning students can be placed either in *Top Notch 1* or *Top Notch Fundamentals*, depending on ability and background. Even absolute beginners can start with confidence in *Top Notch Fundamentals*. False beginners can begin with *Top Notch 1*. The *Top Notch Placement Test* clarifies the best placement within the series.

Estimated teaching time

Each level of *Top Notch* is designed for 60 to 90 instructional hours and contains a full range of supplementary components and enrichment devices to tailor the course to individual needs.

Components of *Top Notch 2*

Student's Book with Take-Home Super CD-ROM

The Super CD-ROM includes a variety of exciting interactive activities: Speaking Practice, Interactive Workbook, Games and Puzzles, and *Top Notch Pop* Karaoke. The disk can also be played on an audio CD player to listen to the Conversation Models and the *Top Notch Pop* songs.

Teacher's Edition and Lesson Planner

Complete yet concise lesson plans are provided for each class. Corpus notes provide essential information from the *Longman Spoken American Corpus* and the *Longman Learner's Corpus*. In addition, a free *Teacher's Resource Disk* offers the following printable extension activities to personalize your teaching style:

- Grammar self-checks
- *Top Notch Pop* song activities
- Writing process worksheets
- Learning strategies
- Pronunciation activities and supplements
- Extra reading comprehension activities
- Vocabulary cards and cumulative vocabulary activities
- Graphic organizers
- Pair work cards

Copy & Go: Ready-made Interactive Activities for Busy Teachers

Interactive games, puzzles, and other practice activities in convenient photocopiable form support the Student's Book content and provide a welcome change of pace.

Complete Classroom Audio Program

The audio program contains listening comprehension activities, rhythm and intonation practice, and targeted pronunciation activities that focus on accurate and comprehensible pronunciation.

Because *Top Notch* prepares students for international communication, a variety of native *and* non-native speakers are included to ready students for the world outside the classroom. The audio program also includes the five *Top Notch Pop* songs in standard and karaoke form.

Workbook

A tightly linked illustrated Workbook contains exercises that provide additional practice and reinforcement of language concepts and skills from *Top Notch* and its Grammar Booster.

Complete Assessment Package with *ExamView*® Software

Ten easy-to-administer and easy-to-score unit achievement tests assess listening, vocabulary, grammar, social language, reading, and writing. Two review tests, one mid-book and one end-of-book, provide additional cumulative assessment. Two speaking tests assess progress in speaking. In addition to the photocopiable achievement tests, *ExamView*® software enables teachers to tailor-make tests to best meet their needs by combining items in any way they wish.

Top Notch TV

A lively and entertaining video offers a TV-style situation comedy that reintroduces language from each *Top Notch* unit, plus authentic unrehearsed interviews with English speakers from around the world and authentic karaoke. Packaged with the video are activity worksheets and a booklet with teaching suggestions and complete video scripts.

Companion Website

A Companion Website at www.longman.com/topnotch provides numerous additional resources for students and teachers. This no-cost, high-benefit feature includes opportunities for further practice of language and content from the *Top Notch* Student's Book.

Welcome to Top Notch!

About the Authors

Joan Saslow

Joan Saslow has taught English as a Foreign Language and English as a Second Language to adults and young adults in both South America and the United States. She taught English and French at the Binational Centers of Valparaíso and Viña del Mar, Chile, and the Catholic University of Valparaíso. In the United States, Ms. Saslow taught English as a Foreign Language to Japanese university students at Marymount College and to international students in Westchester Community College's intensive English program as well as workplace English at the General Motors auto assembly plant in Tarrytown, NY.

Ms. Saslow is the series director of Longman's popular five-level adult series *True Colors: An EFL Course for Real Communication* and of *True Voices*, a five-level video course. She is author of *Ready to Go: Language, Lifeskills, and Civics*, a four-level adult ESL series; *Workplace Plus*, a vocational English series; and of *Literacy Plus*, a two-level series that teaches literacy, English, and culture to adult pre-literate students. She is also author of *English in Context: Reading Comprehension for Science and Technology*, a three-level series for English for special purposes. In addition, Ms. Saslow has been an author, an editor of language teaching materials, a teacher-trainer, and a frequent speaker at gatherings of EFL and ESL teachers for over thirty years.

Allen Ascher

Allen Ascher has been a teacher and teacher-trainer in both China and the United States, as well as an administrator and a publisher. Mr. Ascher specialized in teaching listening and speaking to students at the Beijing Second Foreign Language Institute, to hotel workers at a major international hotel in China, and to Japanese students from Chubu University studying English at Ohio University. In New York, Mr. Ascher taught students of all language backgrounds and abilities at the City University of New York, and he trained teachers in the TESOL Certificate Program at the New School. He was also the academic director of the International English Language Institute at Hunter College.

Mr. Ascher has provided lively workshops for EFL teachers throughout Asia, Latin America, Europe, and the Middle East. He is author of the popular *Think about Editing: A Grammar Editing Guide for ESL Writers*. As a publisher, Mr. Ascher played a key role in the creation of some of the most widely used materials for adults, including: *True Colors, NorthStar, Focus on Grammar, Global Links*, and *Ready to Go*. Mr. Ascher has an M.A. in Applied Linguistics from Ohio University.

Greetings and Small Talk

UNIT GOALS

1 Get reacquainted with someone
2 Greet a visitor to your country
3 Explain local customs
4 Ask about a person's experiences

 A **TOPIC PREVIEW.** Look at the pictures. Do any of the pictures show behavior that would be unusual or strange in your country?

Customs Around the World

Greetings

bow

shake hands

kiss

hug

Exchanging business cards

with two hands

with one hand

Addressing people

Please call me Bill.

Hi, Bill. Call me Pam.

use first names

Hi. I'm Mrs. Song.

I'm Mr. Pike.

use last names

Small talk

So how much money do you make?

ask about salary

So how old are you?

ask about age

So how's your wife?

ask about family

B **DISCUSSION.**

1. How do you prefer to greet and address people?
2. How do you prefer to exchange business cards?
3. When you meet someone new, which subjects are OK to talk about?

☐ the weather   ☐ your age   ☐ your salary   ☐ your family

☐ your job   ☐ your religion   ☐ your home   ☐ other: _____

C 🎧 **SOUND BITES.** Read along silently as you listen to a natural conversation.

ED: You look familiar. Have we met before?
KEITH: I don't think so. I'm not from around here.
ED: Aren't you from Australia, or something like that?
KEITH: As a matter of fact, I am. Keith Lowe.

ED: Ed Santos. I think we met at Jack Bailey's house two weeks ago.
KEITH: Oh, that's right! Now I remember. You're Jack's colleague. What have you been up to?
ED: Not much.

D **PAIR WORK.** Discuss which of the following statements could be true, based on information in the conversation. Explain your decisions.

1. Ed and Keith are friends.
2. Ed is a businessman.
3. Keith is from another country.
4. Ed and Keith met at a party.
5. Ed and Keith both know Jack Bailey.
6. Jack Bailey is Ed's boss.

Sydney Opera House / Australia

WHAT
ABOUT **YOU?**

Which advice would you give a visitor to your country about how to behave? Which advice do you agree with? Which do you disagree with?

It's OK to shake hands, but don't hug people!

Don't ask questions about a person's family.

Never ask about a person's age or salary!

Don't address people by their first names.

Please don't exchange business cards with one hand!

Get Reacquainted with Someone

⌒ CONVERSATION MODEL Read and listen.

A: Audrey, have you met Hanah?

B: No, I haven't.

A: Hanah, I'd like you to meet Audrey.

C: Hi, Audrey. You look familiar. I think we've met before.

B: Really? When?

C: Last month. You were at my sister Nicole's party.

B: Oh, that's right! How have you been?

⌒ Rhythm and intonation practice

 A **GRAMMAR.** The present perfect

GRAMMAR BOOSTER
PAGE G1
For more ...

Use the present perfect to talk about an indefinite time in the past.
Use the simple past tense to talk about a definite time in the past.

present perfect	simple past tense
I**'ve met** Bill twice.	We **met** in 1999 and in 2004.
[indefinite time: We don't know when.]	[definite time: We know when.]

Form the present perfect with <u>have</u> and the past participle form of a verb.

Have you **had** lunch?	Yes, I have. / No, I haven't.
Has she **seen** that new movie?	Yes, she has. / No, she hasn't.

Contractions
've eaten = have eaten
's eaten = has eaten
haven't eaten = have not eaten
hasn't eaten = has not eaten

Regular verbs
The past participle form is the same as the simple past tense form.

simple past tense	past participle
cook**ed**	cook**ed**

Irregular verbs
Look at the list of irregular verbs. For a complete list of irregular
past participle forms, see Appendix, page A5.

Irregular verbs

base form	simple past tense	past participle
be	was / were	been
eat	ate	eaten
go	went	gone
have	had	had
hear	heard	heard
meet	met	met
see	saw	seen
speak	spoke	spoken
take	took	taken
write	wrote	written

 B **Complete each conversation with the present perfect.**

1. (see) **A:** Have you _____ that new Johnny Depp movie?   **B:** Yes, _____.

2. (visit) **A:** Has she _____ Hong Kong?   **B:** No, _____.

3. (meet) **A:** Have you and Mary _____ your new neighbors?   **B:** Yes, _____.

4. (write) **A:** Has your aunt _____ any more letters?   **B:** No, _____.

5. (hear) **A:** Have your friends _____ Sting's new CD?   **B:** Yes, _____.

C Use the present perfect or the simple past tense to complete the conversations.

1. **A:** Have you seen the Taj Mahal?

   B: Yes, I have. I _____ India in 2002. The Taj Mahal _____ fantastic.

visit _____ be

2. **A:** Has the new restaurant opened?

   B: No. It _____. Maybe next week.

open / not

3. **A:** Have you eaten dinner?

   B: No, I haven't. But I _____ a big lunch only two hours ago.

eat

4. **A:** Have they bought their tickets?

   B: I think so. They _____ to the travel agency last week.

go

5. **A:** Have you met the new teacher?

   B: No. The class _____.

start / not

6. **A:** Has your daughter been to Europe?

   B: Well, she _____ to the U.K. last year. But she _____

go _____ be / not
   to any other countries.

CONVERSATION PAIR WORK

Introduce classmates. If you think you've met before, get reacquainted. Or use the pictures to role-play where you may have met. Start like this:

A: _____, have you met _____?
B: _____ …
C: _____ …

in a class

at a theater

at a gym

at a friend's house

at an art exhibition

2 ▸ *Greet a Visitor to Your Country*

Sugarloaf, Rio de Janeiro

CONVERSATION MODEL Read and listen.

A: Welcome to Rio. Have you ever been here before?

B: No. It's my first time. But yesterday I went to Sugarloaf. It was really beautiful.

A: That's great. Have you tried feijoada yet?

B: Feijoada? No, I haven't. What's that?

A: It's a famous Brazilian dish. I think you'll like it.

Feijoada

Rhythm and intonation practice

A ⌒ **VOCABULARY.** Tourist activities around the world. **Listen and practice.**

climb Mt. Fuji

go sightseeing in New York

go to the top of the Eiffel Tower

try Korean food

take a tour of the Tower of London

take pictures of the Great Wall

B ▸ **What have <u>you</u> done?** Use the vocabulary. ❝ I've climbed… ❞ ❝ I've gone sightseeing in… ❞

C ▸ **GRAMMAR.** The present perfect with <u>yet</u>, <u>already</u>, <u>ever</u>, and <u>before</u>

Use <u>yet</u> at the end of questions in the present perfect to ask about recent experiences.
   Have you seen the Pyramids **yet**? Has she tried Thai food **yet**?

Use <u>already</u> in affirmative statements. Use <u>yet</u> in negative statements.
   I've **already** tried sushi. But I haven't tried sashimi **yet**.

Use <u>ever</u> and <u>before</u> in questions to ask about someone's life experiences.
   Has Helen **ever** been to London? Has she been to London **before**?
   Have you **ever** eaten feijoada? Have you **ever** eaten feijoada **before**?

GRAMMAR BOOSTER

PAGES G2–G3
For more …

D Use the words to write statements or questions in the present perfect.

1. you / go sightseeing / in London / before _____?
2. she / already / try / Guatemalan food _____.
3. they / ever / be / to Buenos Aires _____?
4. we / not take a tour of / Prague / yet _____.
5. she / go to the top of / the Empire State Building / yet _____?

E 🎧 LISTENING COMPREHENSION. Listen and complete the questions in the present perfect. Then listen again and check <u>yes</u> or <u>no</u> to answer each question.

	yes	no
1. Has she _____ the Great Pyramids yet?	☐	☐
2. Has he _____ in Kyoto yet?	☐	☐
3. Has she _____ ceviche yet?	☐	☐
4. Has he _____ the Pyramid of the Sun yet?	☐	☐
5. Has she _____ the Forbidden City yet?	☐	☐

The Great Pyramids / Egypt

A temple in Kyoto / Japan

ceviche / Peru

The Pyramid of the Sun / Mexico City

The Forbidden City / Beijing, China

F PAIR WORK. Write five questions to ask about your partner's life experiences. Write answers to your partner's questions about <u>your</u> life experiences.

Have you ever been to Europe?

Yes, I have. I've been to Germany.

CONVERSATION
PAIR WORK

Write a list of places to see and things to do in this city or town. Then role-play a conversation with a visitor here.

A: Welcome to _____. Have you ever been here before?
B: _____.
A: Really? Have you _____?
B: Well, _____ …

Continue the conversation in your <u>own</u> way.

Places to see:

Things to do:

CONTROLLED PRACTICE

3 *Explain Local Customs*

A **READING WARM-UP.** Which gestures do people use in your country?

"Come with me."

"There he is."

"Six."

B 🎧 **READING.** Read the article about gestures around the world. In your opinion, how are gestures different from speech?

Body Talk!

by Kelly Garbo

To communicate well with people of other countries, you must learn to speak well, right? Yes, but speaking isn't everything. Some experts say only thirty percent of communication comes from talking. Your gestures and other non-verbal actions matter, too.

But in different cultures, the same action can have different meanings. When you have to meet someone from a different culture, be prepared. Do you know what kind of gestures and customs are appropriate?

Let's look at shaking hands. North Americans like a firm handshake. But the French prefer a light, short handshake. If you shake a French person's hand the North American way, he or she may not like it. People in Eastern

European countries and some Latino cultures prefer shorter handshakes, too. Hugging after shaking hands is also a common introduction there. Don't be surprised if a Brazilian gives you a hug. If you misinterpret gestures of introduction, your friendship may get off on the wrong foot!

Everyone around the world knows the "OK" hand gesture, don't they? But in Spain, parts of South America, and Eastern Europe, the OK sign is considered rude. And if you go shopping in Japan, it means you'd like your change in coins instead of bills. In France, making the OK sign means "zero" or that something is worthless. So check before you use the OK sign to be sure it's OK!

Understanding even a few key gestures from different cultures can make you a better communicator. So next time you travel, try being culturally sensitive. Find out the local gesture and let your body talk.

North Americans like a firm handshake.

SOURCE: www.bellaonline.com

C Check the statements that are true, according to Kelly Garbo. Explain why.

☐ **1.** Seventy percent of communication comes from non-verbal actions.

☐ **2.** If you don't speak someone's language, it's always safe to use gestures.

☐ **3.** French people generally don't like firm handshakes.

☐ **4.** Brazilians never shake hands.

☐ **5.** Japanese people think the OK sign is rude.

D **DISCUSSION.** Have you ever been surprised by someone's gestures or non-verbal actions? What was the gesture? What happened?

INTERACTION • *When in Rome . . .*

STEP 1. PAIR WORK. Read the tips about customs around the world. Discuss which ones you've never heard of before.

In the U.S.A., you should call to explain if you're going to be more than 15 minutes late for a party, lunch, or dinner.

In Taiwan, you should cover your mouth when you're using a toothpick.

In Thailand, you should never touch a person, even a child, on the head.

In Saudi Arabia, avoid asking personal questions about a person's family.

In the U.K., it is better not to ask people personal questions, about where they live, how much money they make, or what they do.

In Japan, you should take off your shoes before entering someone's home.

In Russia, wearing a coat in a public building or putting it on a chair in a restaurant is considered rude.

In Ecuador, open a gift immediately and thank the person who gave it to you.

STEP 2. GROUP WORK. Choose a topic. On your notepad, write some rules for how to behave in your country.

Topic:
Rules:
Are there special rules for women?
Are there special rules for children?

Topics
- how to meet and greet new people
- how to behave when you visit someone's home
- how to behave in a restaurant

STEP 3. DISCUSSION. Compare your notes with those of the other groups. Does everyone agree?

FREE PRACTICE

Ask about a Person's Experiences

A 🎧 **LISTENING COMPREHENSION.** Listen to the game show *Once in a Lifetime*. Check if the contestants answered <u>yes</u> or <u>no</u> to the host's questions.

Have you ever...	Suzy		Bill	
	yes	no	yes	no
1. been to South America?	☐	☐	☐	☐
2. been to China?	☐	☐	☐	☐
3. flown in an airplane?	☐	☐	☐	☐
4. driven a bus?	☐	☐	☐	☐
5. bought a digital camera?	☐	☐	☐	☐
6. visited Chicago?	☐	☐	☐	☐

Once in a Lifetime with Pete Sosa

Have you ever...?

Pete Sosa

Suzy

Bill

B 🎧 **Now listen again and answer the questions.**

1. Where does Suzy live? Where does Bill live?
2. What does Suzy do? What does Bill do?
3. Where has Suzy been in South America?
4. Where has Suzy flown in an airplane?

C **DISCUSSION.** How would <u>you</u> answer each of the questions from the game show?

D 🎧 **PRONUNCIATION.** Negative contractions. Notice how the /t/ sound of the negative contraction "disappears." Listen and repeat.

1. We haven't visited Rio.
2. He hasn't met his new boss.
3. They haven't been to Asia.
4. She hasn't eaten dinner yet.

INTERACTION • *Getting to know you*

STEP 1. PAIR WORK. Take the survey. Check the experiences <u>you've</u> had and compare your answers with your partner's. Discuss the details of each experience.

1. Have you ever tried...?

 ☐ snake

 ☐ octopus

 ☐ guinea pig

 ☐ Swiss cheese

2. Have you ever been to...?

 ☐ Moscow

 ☐ Shanghai

 ☐ Istanbul

 ☐ Honolulu

3. Have you ever gone...?

 ☐ hang gliding

 ☐ sailing

 ☐ horseback riding

 ☐ snorkeling

How many boxes did you check?

9–12	Daredevil	Your life is just too exciting!
5–8	Go-getter	You're a real adventurer!
1–4	Fence-sitter	You're ready for more!
0	Scaredy-cat	You really should do something new!

STEP 2. WRITING. Write about an experience from the survey. Or write about what you've never done, but would like to do.

STEP 3. Walk around the room and ask your classmates questions. Complete the chart.

Find someone who has ...	Name	What this person has done ...
1. lived in another country.		
2. met a famous person.		
3. learned to play an instrument.		
4. eaten something unusual.		
5. done something dangerous.		

STEP 4. GROUP WORK. Choose a classmate from the chart. Introduce that person to your class.

❝This is Sylvia. She's learned to play two instruments: the piano and the guitar.❞

dim sum

A 🎧 **LISTENING COMPREHENSION.** **Listen to the conversation with a tourist in Vancouver. Check <u>yes</u> or <u>no</u>.**

	Has she...	yes	no
1.	been to the Vancouver Aquarium yet?	☐	☐
2.	been to the top of Grouse Mountain?	☐	☐
3.	visited Gastown yet?	☐	☐
4.	tried dim sum yet?	☐	☐
5.	gone to the top of the Harbor Center Tower?	☐	☐
6.	seen the Capilano Suspension Bridge yet?	☐	☐

the Vancouver Aquarium

B **Use the pictures to write questions. Don't use the same verb more than once. Use the present perfect with <u>ever</u> or <u>before</u>.**

Example: <u>Have you ever visited the Korean Folk Village in Yong-in, Korea</u> ?

1. _____?
2. _____?
3. _____?
4. _____?

The Tower of Pisa / Italy

Thai food

Mount Aconcagua / Argentina

London / U.K.

Korean Folk Village / Yong-in, Korea

C **WRITING.** **On a separate sheet of paper, write a paragraph introducing yourself to your class. Tell about some unusual experiences you've had.**

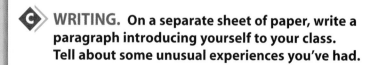

My name is Lee. I've never been to London, but...

 TOP NOTCH SONG
"Greetings and Small Talk"
Lyrics on last page before Workbook.

TOP NOTCH PROJECT
Write a guide for a visitor to this country. Include tips to explain how to behave and how NOT to behave.

 TOP NOTCH WEBSITE
For Unit 1 online activities, visit the *Top Notch* Companion Website at www.longman.com/topnotch.

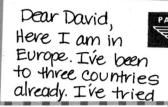

Dear David,
Here I am in
Europe. I've been
to three countries
already. I've tried

David Linder
330 West Pike Street
Vancouver, B.C.
CANADA V5K 2M8

UNIT WRAP-UP

- **Social Language.** Create conversations for the tourists.

  Welcome to Paris. Have you been here before?

- **Writing.** Write a postcard from a tourist in the picture. Describe the things you have done.

UNITED KINGDOM

the Millennium Wheel

Buckingham Palace

London

E U R O P E

Mozart's house

Vienna Boys' Choir

Vienna

AUSTRIA

Paris

the Eiffel Tower

crepes

FRANCE

the Campanile Tower

Venice

a gondola

ITALY

ATLANTIC OCEAN

the Prado Museum

Madrid

tapas

SPAIN

M E D I T E R R A N E A N   S E A

GREECE

the Parthenon

moussaka

Athens

✔ Now I can ...

- ☐ get reacquainted with someone.
- ☐ greet a visitor to my country.
- ☐ explain local customs.
- ☐ ask about a person's experiences.

N
W   E
S

Movies and Entertainment

UNIT GOALS

1 Apologize for lateness
2 Discuss preferences
3 Compare tastes in movies
4 Discuss the effect of violence on viewers

 TOPIC PREVIEW. Do you rent videos or DVDs? Read the descriptions of two popular films in a movie catalog.

The Movie Lover's Catalog

If you love movies, you absolutely MUST have our catalog. It's the largest source of movies on video available in the world today. From the classics of the 30s to musicals of the Golden Age of Hollywood—and everything since—you can't beat The Movie Lover's Catalog. We have a new and expanded inventory of international films, Japanese animations, drama, comedies—even classic and current TV shows!

Frida [DVD] (2002)
Mexican painter Frida Kahlo's life is brought to the screen by director Julie Taymor and producer/star Salma Hayek. Kahlo's story is traced from her teens all the way through her complex relationship with painter husband Diego Rivera (Alfred Molina). Kahlo's search for her own identity in her paintings is covered in vivid color and with great sensitivity. Ashley Judd, Antonio Banderas, Geoffrey Rush, and Edward Norton also star.

DIRECTOR: Julie Taymor   **CATEGORY:** Drama

The Day the Earth Stood Still [VHS] (1951)
All sci-fi drama buffs will want to own this classic sci-fi drama with a message. Michael Rennie stars as Klaatu, a visitor from the stars who arrives on Earth with his robot companion, Gort. Klaatu's mission is to warn mankind about the danger of nuclear warfare. Patricia Neal, Sam Jaffe, Billy Gray also star; Robert Wise directs.

DIRECTOR: Robert Wise   **CATEGORY:** Sci-Fi & Fantasy

Also available on DVD

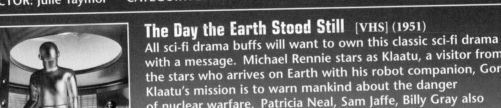

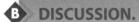 **DISCUSSION.**

1. Where would you rather see a movie: at home or in the theater? Why?

2. Have you ever seen *Frida* or *The Day the Earth Stood Still*? Which movie would you rather rent? Explain your choice.

C 🎧 **SOUND BITES.** Read along silently as you listen to a natural conversation.

All Classics All the Time
THEATER
Some Like It Hot (Comedy)
Frida (Drama)
Chicago (Musical)
Star Wars (Sci-Fi)
Dracula (Horror)

LISA: You're going to love this theater. You can see all the things you missed.
DAN: I'm really in the mood for a good classic movie. And on a big screen!
LISA: Much better than on the tube.

DAN: You know, I never saw *Frida*. Did you?
LISA: No. I missed it.
DAN: They say it was great. How about it?
LISA: Actually, I'd rather see something else…. Hey! They're showing *Dracula*!
DAN: Deal!

D Check the statements that are true. Explain your answers.

☐ **1.** The theater shows old movies.
☐ **2.** Dan prefers to rent a video rather than go to the movies.

☐ **3.** Lisa has already seen *Frida*.
☐ **4.** Dan's not in the mood for *Frida*.
☐ **5.** They decide to see *Dracula*.

E **IN OTHER WORDS.** With a partner, restate each statement in your own words.

1. "I'm in the mood for a good classic movie."
2. "Much better than on the tube."

3. "I missed it."
4. "Deal!"

WHAT ABOUT **YOU?**

PAIR WORK. Check the genres you like best. Then discuss movies that you've seen in each genre.

☐ comedy   ☐ musical   ☐ drama   ☐ action   ☐ science fiction ("sci-fi")

1 ▷ *Apologize for Lateness*

 ☐ CONVERSATION MODEL Read and listen.

A: Sorry I'm late. Have you been here long?

B: For about 10 minutes. Not too bad.

A: I'm sorry. I got stuck in traffic.

B: The 8:00 show for *The Train* is sold out, so I got tickets for *High Flyer*. I hope that's OK.

A: That's fine. They say it's hilarious. How much do I owe?

B: Nothing. It's on me.

A: Well, thanks. Next time it's my treat.

☐ Rhythm and intonation practice

A ▷ **GRAMMAR.** The present perfect: additional uses

Use since with a time or date in the past.

How long have you lived here? I've lived here **since 2001**.

Use for to describe a period of time.

How long have you lived here? I've lived here **for five years**.

Other uses:

with always: I've **always** wanted to see *Gone with the Wind*.

with ordinals, the superlative, or only: This is **the third time** I've seen *Frida*. It's **the best** movie I've ever seen. My husband has **only** seen it once.

with lately / recently, just: Have you seen a good movie **lately**? Yes. I've **just** seen *Seabiscuit*.

with still, so far: You **still** haven't seen *Chicago*? I've seen it three times **so far**!

GRAMMAR BOOSTER

PAGES G3–G4
For more ...

B ▷ Complete the biography of Spanish actor Antonio Banderas. Use **for** or **since**.

Banderas has acted _____ more than 20 years. He has worked in
1.
the theater _____ 1982, and he has acted in films _____ 1992. *The*
2.   3.
Mambo Kings Sing Songs of Love was his first film in English, but
Banderas didn't speak English at that time, and he had to read
his script phonetically. Banderas has had an international
reputation _____ 1988, when he appeared in *Women on the*
4.
Verge of a Nervous Breakdown. Banderas met his wife, Melanie
Griffith, on the set of *Two Much*, and they have been married
_____ over eight years. _____ their daughter, Stella, was
5.   6.
born, they have lived in Los Angeles and Spain.

PAIR WORK. Take turns asking and answering the following questions. Use the present perfect in your answers.

> 66 I've always wanted to see Hitchcock's *The Birds.* 99

1. Is there a movie you've always wanted to see?
2. Have you seen any good movies recently?
3. What's the best movie you've ever seen?
4. What's the worst movie you've ever seen?
5. How many movies have you seen so far this month?

 🎧 **PRONUNCIATION.** Reduction of /h/. Notice how the /h/ sound "disappears." Listen and repeat.

1. How long have you lived here?
2. Where have you worked?
3. When did he leave?
4. What's her name?

 🎧 **VOCABULARY.** Some explanations for being late. Listen and practice.

I got stuck in traffic.

I missed the bus.

I couldn't get a taxi.

I couldn't find a parking space.

 Write two other explanations for being late.

_____ _____

CONVERSATION
PAIR WORK

Apologize for being late meeting a friend at the movies. Provide an explanation. Then, together, use the schedule to decide on a movie to see.
Start like this:

A: Sorry I'm late. Have you been here long?

B: For _____ ...

War of the Planets	7:30	9:35	[7:30 sold out]
Love Me in Lima	7:45	10:20	midnight
Kitten Story	8:00	11:00	[8:00 sold out]
Better Late Than Never	7:50	10:10	

Discuss Preferences

🎧 CONVERSATION
MODEL Read and listen.

A: What would you rather see—a comedy or a musical?

B: It doesn't matter to me.

A: Well, what do you think of Madonna?

B: Actually, not much.

A: For real? She's my favorite movie star.

B: Not mine.

A: Well, that's what makes the world go 'round!

🎧 **Rhythm and intonation practice**

☹
Not much.
I don't like _____.
I can't stand _____.

☺
I love _____.
_____ 's great!

A 🎧 **VOCABULARY.** Movie genres. Listen and practice.

an action film

a horror film

a science-fiction film

an animated film

a comedy

a documentary

a drama

a musical

B **PAIR WORK.** Compare your favorite movies for each genre.

C 🎧 **LISTENING COMPREHENSION.** Listen to the movie reviews and recommendations. Then use the movie genre vocabulary to complete the chart.

Movie title	Genre	Recommended?	
		yes	no
Hot Dog			
First Things First			
Aqua-technia			
The Wolf Children			

D **DISCUSSION.** Which movies sound good to <u>you</u>? Listen again if necessary. Explain.

E GRAMMAR. _Would rather_ ───────────────

State preferences with <u>would rather</u> / <u>would rather not</u> and the base form of a verb.

I'**d rather rent** a movie than go to the theater.
He'**d rather not see** a comedy tonight.

I'**d rather** = I would rather

Questions

Would you **rather** see _Star Wars_ or _Frida_?
Which **would** they **rather** see—a comedy or a drama?
Would you like to rent a movie? Actually, we'**d rather not**. We're too busy.

F Complete each conversation with <u>would rather</u> or <u>would rather not</u>.

1. "I'd love to see a good movie tonight."

YOU Actually, _I'd rather stay home_ _____.

2. "I'm in the mood for a horror film."

YOU Actually, _____.

3. "Why don't we get tickets for the late show?"

YOU Actually, _____.

4. "Ben told me you wanted to rent a movie."

YOU Actually, _____.

5. "Would you like to see a comedy?"

YOU Actually, _____.

6. "How about some Italian food after the movie?"

YOU Actually, _____.

CONVERSATION
PAIR WORK

Make a list of your favorite movies and movie stars. Then choose a movie to see. Use the guide, or create a <u>new</u> conversation.

A: What would you rather see: _____ or _____?
B: It doesn't matter to me.
A: Well, what do you think of _____?
B: Actually, _____.
A: _____ …

Continue the conversation in your <u>own</u> way.

My favorite movies:

My favorite movie stars:

CONTROLLED PRACTICE

19

3 ▶ Compare Tastes in Movies

A 🎧 **VOCABULARY.** Adjectives to describe movies. **Listen and practice.**

funny: something that makes you laugh

romantic: about love

boring: not interesting

weird: very strange or unusual, in a negative way

violent: containing a lot of fighting and killing

unforgettable: something that you will always remember

silly: not serious; almost stupid

B **PAIR WORK.** **Write a movie you know for each adjective. Compare your choices.**

a funny movie:	a violent movie:
a romantic movie:	an unforgettable movie:
a boring movie:	a silly movie:
a weird movie:	

C 🎧 **LISTENING COMPREHENSION.** **Listen carefully to a conversation between two people reading movie reviews from the newspaper. Choose the adjective from the vocabulary that best represents their opinions.**

romantic

D 🎧 **Listen again. Which movies do they like? Which movies do they think are bad?**

INTERACTION • *Movie reviews*

STEP 1. PAIR WORK. Read the capsule movie reviews of four classic movies. Use <u>would rather</u> to talk about which movie you'd like to see. Explain why.

BEND IT LIKE BECKHAM

✪✪✪ ¹/2 (PG-13, 112 minutes). An Indian girl (Parminder K. Nagra) living in London wants to play pro soccer, but her traditional Sikh parents want her to marry a nice Indian boy. Just about the perfect teenage coming-of-age comedy.

Finding Nemo

✪✪✪✪ (G, 101 minutes). A little clown fish gets lost, and his dad and another fish team up to find him. Visually beautiful, an adventure for kids plus a humorous level adults will appreciate.

The Heart of Me

✪✪✪ (R, 96 minutes). Helena Bonham Carter stars as a woman who has the misfortune to fall in love with the husband (Paul Bettany) of her sister (Olivia Williams). Portrays London society, circa 1940.

Spellbound

✪✪✪ (Unrated, suitable for all, 95 minutes). This Oscar-nominated U.S. documentary visits the homes of eight finalists for the National Spelling Bee, and then follows them to the finals in Washington. We get to know the kids and their families.

Source: Roger Ebert's One-Minute Reviews in the *Chicago Sun-Times*

STEP 2. On your notepad, make notes about two movies you've seen recently.

Title:	Title:
Genre:	Genre:
Stars:	Stars:
What is the movie about?	What is the movie about?
Adjectives:	Adjectives:

STEP 3. DISCUSSION. Talk about movies you've seen recently.

"Was it good?"   *"Do you recommend it?"*

"Who was in it?"

"What kind of movie was it?"   *"What was it about?"*

4 Discuss the Effect of Violence on Viewers

A **READING WARM-UP.** Are violent movies good entertainment, or can they be dangerous?

B 🎧 **READING.** Read the article about violence in movies. Which opinions do you agree with?

Can Violent Movies Be Dangerous?

Before the 1960s, most movies did not show much graphic violence. When fighting or shooting occurred on the screen, it was clean: Bang! You're dead! The victim fell to the ground and died, perhaps after speaking a few final words. The viewer never saw blood or suffering. But in the late '60s, filmmakers Arthur Penn and Sam Peckinpah began making movies with more graphic violence, such as *Bonnie and Clyde* and *The Wild Bunch.* They believed that if audiences could see how truly horrible real violence was, people would be less violent in their own lives.

Today, special effects technology has made it possible to create very realistic images of bloodshed and violence. Steven Prince, author of *Savage Cinema: Sam Peckinpah and the Rise of Ultraviolent Movies,* describes the difference between early movies and the movies of today "…filmmakers can create any image that they can dream up." So, Prince believes, because of the technology, movies today have become more and more violent and bloody.

Some people are worried that viewing a lot of violence in movies and video games can be dangerous. They feel that it can make violence seem normal and can cause people to imitate the violent behavior, to do the same thing themselves. Other people disagree. They believe that showing violence is honest and can even be helpful.

One popular filmmaker asks why violent images on the screen

Bonnie & Clyde

are a problem since we live in such a violent world. "Just open any newspaper," he says. "Any newspaper is much more violent. And those are true stories about what happens in real life. Or open any history book and read about what happens when a people are conquered."

"There's so much violence right now," says a well-known European actress. "And maybe this is the way that filmmakers speak against violence: by making violent movies."

The Wild Bunch

C Check the statements that are true, according to the article.

☐ **1.** Movies have always been very violent.
☐ **2.** Graphic violence has been common since *Bonnie and Clyde* and *The Wild Bunch.*
☐ **3.** Peckinpah and Penn thought that violence on the screen can never be good.
☐ **4.** Peckinpah and Penn thought that violent movies would make people behave more violently in their own lives.
☐ **5.** Everyone agrees that graphic violence on the movie screen is OK.

D **PAIR WORK.** With a partner, find a statement in the article to support each of your answers in Exercise C.

INTERACTION • *Where do YOU stand?*

STEP 1. **Complete the chart with films and television shows you know. Rate the level of violence from 0 to 3, with 3 being the most violent.**

TITLE	MEDIUM	LEVEL OF VIOLENCE
Bonnie and Clyde	film	2

0 = not violent   1 = somewhat violent
2 = violent   3 = ultra violent

STEP 2. **PAIR WORK.** **On your notepad, make notes about the most violent film or show on your chart. Tell your partner about it.**

	Title:
	What's it about?
	Is it dangerous for some viewers?
	Why? Why not?

STEP 3. **DISCUSSION.**

1. Have movies become more violent in your lifetime? What are some examples of very violent movies?

2. Do people imitate the behavior they see in the movies? Can movies make people violent? Who should not see violent movies?

3. Can violence in other media, such as books and newspapers, also be dangerous?

> **I think** *Bonnie and Clyde* is dangerous **because** when some people see it, it's possible that they will rob banks too.

> **I disagree.** Movies are not dangerous.

> **I feel** some movies are too dangerous for children.

> **I agree.** Children imitate everything.

STEP 4. **WRITING.** **Write a short article expressing your opinion about violence in movies and on TV.**

FREE PRACTICE

UNIT 2
CHECKPOINT

A 🎧 **LISTENING COMPREHENSION.** Listen carefully to the conversations about movies. Decide which adjective best represents each speaker's opinion.

1. *Mediterranean Moon* is _____.

2. *The Violinist* was _____.

3. *The Good Catch* was _____.

4. *My Neighbors on Neptune* is _____.

5. *Plants of the Kalahari* is _____.

6. *Animal Opera* is _____.

7. *Crazy Horse* was _____.

unforgettable
boring
silly
weird
funny
romantic
violent

B Read the DVD box labels. Then write the genre of each movie.

1. _____

2. _____

3. _____

4. _____

C Write your own response to each statement or question.

1. "Sorry I'm late."

   YOU _____.

2. "How long have you been here?"

   YOU _____.

3. "I rented *Murder at Midnight*. I hope that's OK."

   YOU _____.

4. "You bought the tickets? How much do I owe?"

   YOU _____.

5. "Next time it's my treat."

   YOU _____.

D Complete each statement or question with **for** or **since**.

1. That film has played at the Metroplex _____ two weeks.

2. *The Talking Parrot* has been available on DVD _____ last Tuesday.

3. I've loved the movies _____ I was a child.

4. Have you been here _____ more than an hour?

🎧 *TOP NOTCH SONG*
"Better Late Than Never"
Lyrics on last page before Workbook.

TOP NOTCH **PROJECT**
Create a movie review page with your class. Write reviews about good and bad movies.

TOP NOTCH **WEBSITE**
For Unit 2 online activities, visit the *Top Notch* Companion Website at www.longman.com/topnotch.

Cult of Blood
7:20 9:00 midnight
(sold out)

Love in Paradise
7:15 9:45

Ticket to the Moon
8:00 10:00

UNIT WRAP-UP

- **Social language.** Create conversations for the people.

  A: How long have you been here?
  B: About 20 minutes.

- **Writing.** Write about the picture.

  A man and woman are looking at the movie posters...

7:30

Ticket to the Moon

Love in Paradise

Cult of Blood

✓ *Now I can ...*

☐ apologize for lateness.
☐ discuss preferences.
☐ compare tastes in movies.
☐ discuss the effect of violence on viewers.

25

Staying at Hotels

UNIT GOALS

1 Leave and take a message
2 Check in
3 Request housekeeping services
4 Choose a hotel

 TOPIC PREVIEW. Look at the hotel bill. How many nights did the guest stay at the hotel?

Hotel del Mundo
Paseo de la Castellana 112, Madrid, Spain

Ms. Soo-Jin Hong
Paradise Apt. #105-511
Myungil-dong, Gangdong-gu
Seoul, Korea 134-756

ROOM	1102
ARRIVAL	19/01/06
DEPARTURE	25/01/06
TIME	15:52

DATE	REFERENCE	DESCRIPTION	AMOUNT
19/01	09562	Limousine	19.00
19/01	00:06:22	Overseas Call #1102	2.50
19/01		Room #1102	75.00
20/01	00:00:10	Local Call #1102	.25
20/01		Coffee Shop	7.90
20/01	130354	Internet access 15 mins.	3.00
20/01	130356	Internet access 15 mins.	3.00
20/01		Room #1102	75.00
21/01	130356	Photocopies	47.63
21/01		Minibar #1102	2.85
21/01		Coffee Shop	5.50
21/01	00:00:08	Local Call #1102	.25
21/01		Room #1102	75.00
22/01	00:00:04	Local Call #1102	.25
22/01	00:31:10	Overseas Call #1102	12.90
22/01		Room #1102	75.00
23/01		Minibar #1102	5.00
23/01		Coffee Shop	6.94
23/01	00:30:40	Overseas Call #1102	12.50
23/01		Room #1102	75.00
24/01		Minibar #1102	1.00
24/01		Room #1102	75.00
25/01		Coffee Shop	5.10
25/01	09563	Limousine	19.00
		BALANCE	604.57 (Euro)

TOTAL INCLUDING VAT*   645.46 (Euro)

GUEST SIGNATURE _____ *Soo-Jin Hong* _____

*VAT=Value Added Tax

1. INSERT CARD FIRMLY
2. PUSH DOWN HANDLE
3. OPEN DOOR
4. REMOVE CARD

Hotel del Mundo
1102

 DISCUSSION.

1. How much did the guest pay in Euros for the total bill, including tax?
2. How many phone calls did the guest make? How many times did the guest use the Internet?
3. What other services did the guest use?

 OPTION: Check the newspaper or the Internet to convert Euros to your local currency.

D 🎧 **SOUND BITES.** Read along silently as you listen to a conversation in a hotel in Spain.

GUEST: Good morning. I'm checking out. Here's my key card.

CLERK: Was your stay satisfactory?

GUEST: Yes. Very nice, thanks.

CLERK: Did you have anything from the minibar last night?

GUEST: Yes. Two bottles of spring water.

CLERK: And will you be putting this on your Vista card?

GUEST: Yes, I will.

CLERK: Here you go, ma'am. Thank you for staying with us. Will you need a taxi?

GUEST: Yes, please.

E Check the statements that are true. Explain your answers.

☐ **1.** The guest is leaving the hotel.

☐ **2.** The guest asks for spring water.

☐ **3.** The guest pays cash.

☐ **4.** The guest is going to the airport.

WHAT ABOUT **YOU?**

Which hotel services would you use?

 ☐ room service

 ☐ minibar

 ☐ Internet connection

 ☐ photocopying

 ☐ laundry

 ☐ shoe shine

 ☐ airport shuttle

☐ other _____

 It's 6:00 a.m. ☐ wake-up service

 ☐ babysitting

 ☐ bell service

1 Leave and Take a Message

CONVERSATION
MODEL Read and listen.

A: Hello? I'd like to speak to Anne Smith. She's a guest.

B: I'll ring that room for you.

• • •

B: I'm sorry. She's not answering. Would you like to leave a message?

A: Yes. Please tell her Tim Klein called. I'll meet her at the hotel at three this afternoon.

B: Is that all?

A: Yes, thanks.

Rhythm and intonation practice

Some messages
Please tell her I'll call back later.
Please tell her I'll be at the Clayton Hotel until 5:00.
Please tell her I'll be at 22-56-838.

A **GRAMMAR. The future with will**

Use will and the base form of a verb to talk about the future.

She'**ll be** back in an hour.   OK. I'**ll call** her later.

Negative statements

I **won't call** before noon.

Questions

Will you **come** at 6:00?   Yes, I will. / No, I won't.
When **will** Gary **arrive**?   At 10:00.

Remember: You can also talk about the future with <u>be going to</u>, the present continuous, or the simple present tense.

I'**m going to** leave a message.
We'**re meeting** at 3:00.
They **arrive** tomorrow.

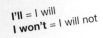

I'll = I will
I won't = I will not

GRAMMAR BOOSTER

PAGE G5
For more …

B **Rewrite the following future statements and questions, using <u>will</u>.**

1. I'm going to call her later today. _____ *I'll call her later today* _____.

2. She's going to stop at the front desk first. _____.

3. My uncle is meeting my father at the airport. _____.

4. What time does the tour group get back? _____?

5. When are they going to make a reservation? _____?

6. Where is your grandmother staying in Madrid? _____?

C ○ LISTENING COMPREHENSION. Listen to the phone messages. Complete each message slip, according to the information you hear.

IMPORTANT MESSAGE

FOR: _____Judy Diller_____

☑ Mr. / ☐ Ms. / ☐ Mrs. / ☐ Miss _____Marc Pearl_____

Phone number: _____

☐ Telephoned   ☐ Please call
☐ Came to see you   ☐ Will call again
☐ Wants to see you   ☐ Returned your call

Message: _____
_____
_____

🔔 **PHONE MESSAGE**

FOR: _____Hank Pitt_____

☐ Mr. / ☑ Ms. / ☐ Mrs. / ☐ Miss _____

Phone: _____

☐ Please call   ☐ Will call again
☐ Wants to see you   ☐ Returned your call

Message: _____
_____
_____

A Message For You

FOR: _____Collin Mack_____

☐ Mr. / ☑ Ms. / ☐ Mrs. / ☐ Miss _____

Phone: _____

☐ Called   ☐ Please call back
☐ Came to see you   ☐ Will call back
☐ Wants to meet   ☐ Returned your call

Message: _____

||||||||||||||||||||||||||||||||||||||||||||||||

WHILE YOU WERE OUT...

FOR: _____Patricia Carlton_____

☑ Mr. / ☐ Ms. / ☐ Mrs. / ☐ Miss _____ called.

Phone: _____

☐ Please call back
☐ Will call again

Message: _____
_____
_____

D ○ PRONUNCIATION. Contractions with will. Notice that each contraction is one syllable. Listen and repeat.

1. I'll call back later.
2. She'll be at the Clayton Hotel.
3. He'll use his credit card.
4. We'll need a limousine.
5. You'll get the bill in the mail.
6. They'll meet you at 6:00.

CONVERSATION
PAIR WORK

Role-play a phone call. Take a message on the message pad.

A: Hello? I'd like to speak to _____.

B: I'm sorry. _____. Would you like to leave a message?

A: Yes. _____ ...

Continue the conversation in your own way.

||||||||||||||||||||||||||||||||||||||||||||

WHILE YOU WERE OUT ...

FOR: _____

☐ Mr. / ☐ Ms. / ☐ Mrs. / ☐ Miss _____ called.

Phone: _____
☐ Please call back
☐ Will call again
Message: _____
_____

CONTROLLED PRACTICE

29

2 ▶ *Check in*

🎧 CONVERSATION
MODEL **Read and listen.**

A: Hi. I'm checking in. The name's Baker.
B: Let's see. That's one double for two nights. Non-smoking?
A: That's right.
B: How do you want to pay?
A: Here's my card. By the way, is the restaurant still open?
B: Actually, you'd better hurry. It closes at 9:00.

🎧 **Rhythm and intonation practice**

A 🎧 **VOCABULARY.** **Hotel room features.**
Listen and practice.

a single room

a double room

a suite

a twin bed

a queen-size bed

a king-size bed

smoking non-smoking

a rollaway bed

🎧 **LISTENING COMPREHENSION. Listen carefully to the conversations. Write the hotel room features the guest needs. Listen again and check your answers.**

1. _____ 2. _____ 3. _____ 4. _____

_____   _____   _____   _____

_____   _____   _____   _____

C **GRAMMAR. Had better** ―――――――――――――――――――――

Use <u>had better</u> to warn someone about a possible negative result.

You'**d better hurry**! You'll be late.

She'**d better make** a reservation soon. That hotel is very popular.

Negative statements

We'**d better not be** late.

Note: The contraction <u>'d better</u> is almost always used in spoken English.

GRAMMAR BOOSTER

PAGES G6–G7
For more …

D **Complete each conversation with <u>had better</u> or <u>had better not</u>. Use contractions.**

1. **A:** Is the museum very far from here?

   B: Yes, it is. You _____ take a taxi.

2. **A:** When does the meeting begin?

   B: Two o'clock sharp. We _____ be late.

3. **A:** It looks like rain.

   B: Well, you _____ walk. Take the bus instead.

4. **A:** It's already 9:30! I'm starving.

   B: Well, the restaurant closes at 10:30.
   We _____ hurry.

CONVERSATION
PAIR WORK

**Role-play checking in. Discuss the room features you want.
Ask about the hotel facilities in the pictures.**

A: Hi. I'm checking in. The name's _____.

B: _____ …

Continue the conversation in your <u>own</u> way.

HOURS
9 a.m. to 5 p.m.

business center

HOURS
6 a.m. to 10 p.m.

pool

HOURS
6 a.m. to 9 p.m.

fitness center

HOURS
11 a.m. to 8 p.m.

sauna

HOURS
8:00 to 21:00

gift shop

3 Request Housekeeping Services

A 🎧 **VOCABULARY.** Hotel room amenities and services. **Listen and practice.**

We need ...

extra towels.

extra hangers.

skirt hangers.

an iron.

a hair dryer.

Could someone ...

make up the room?

turn down the beds?

pick up the laundry?

bring up a newspaper?

take away the dishes?

B 🎧 **LISTENING COMPREHENSION.** Listen to the two phone conversations with the hotel staff. Then listen again and check the hotel services or items each guest is requesting.

Room 586		
☐ turn down the beds	☐ take away the dishes	☐ bring extra hangers
☐ bring an iron	☐ pick up the laundry	☐ bring a hair dryer
☐ bring extra towels	☐ bring skirt hangers	☐ make up the room

Room 587		
☐ turn down the beds	☐ take away the dishes	☐ bring extra hangers
☐ bring an iron	☐ pick up the laundry	☐ bring a hair dryer
☐ bring extra towels	☐ bring skirt hangers	☐ make up the room

INTERACTION • *I'll take care of that right away!*

STEP 1. PAIR WORK. Choose a guest. Tell your partner what the guest is saying.

STEP 2. Role-play telephone conversations between one of the guests and a hotel front desk clerk. Use the pictures or other ideas.

NEED HELP?

Here's language you
already know:

Hotel Guest	Front Desk Clerk
We need ____.	Can I help you?
Could someone ____?	What's the problem?
Is the ____ still open?	I'm sorry to hear that.
What time does the ____ close?	How is / was the ____?
I'd like ____.	Let me check.
I'd like to ____.	Certainly.
That would be great.	You'd better hurry.

4 Choose a Hotel

A ▶ **READING WARM-UP.** What is the most important factor for you in choosing a hotel—price, location, etc.?

B ▶ 🎧 **READING.** Read the hotel guide for New York City. Which hotel sounds attractive to you?

New York City has some of the best hotels in the world—and, believe it or not, some are not too expensive. But here are our picks for "the best of the best."

$$$$	Very expensive
$$$	Expensive
$$	Moderately priced
$	Budget

Most famous hotel
The Plaza Hotel $$$
768 Fifth Ave. (at 59th St.)
800 441-1414
805 rooms

Located at the southeast corner of New York's fabulous Central Park, The Plaza is as near as it gets to the best shopping along New York's famous Fifth Avenue. This 1907 hotel, with its beautiful fountain, is a famous location in many popular movies and books. Movie stars and the rich love to get married there. *4 restaurants, excellent full-service spa and health club, concierge and ticket desk, car-rental desk, business center, 24-hour room service, babysitting, laundry*

SOURCE: Adapted from *Frommer's New York City 2003*

Best service at a low price
The Broadway Inn $$
264 W. 46th St. (at Eighth Ave.)
800 826-6300
41 rooms
Impeccably clean and very comfortable, this hotel is a real winner. Suites can be a great deal—with sofa, microwave, mini-fridge and lots of closet space. Located right in the noisy Theater District, the hotel is peaceful and quiet inside. Best of all are the attentive staff who work hard to make their guests happy. There is a special phone number in case guests have questions while they're out sightseeing. Note: This four-story hotel has no elevators.
2 restaurants next door, concierge, fax and copy service

Most interesting hotel
Hotel Chelsea $$
222 W. 23rd St. (between Seventh and Eighth Aves.) 212 243-3700
400 rooms, 100 available to travelers

If you're looking for the usual hotel comforts, go elsewhere. But if you're looking for atmosphere—the New York of artists, actors, and writers—this is the only place to stay. Well-known novels and plays were written here. And artists and writers live here even today. This 1884 Victorian hotel has beautiful cast-iron balconies and a busy lobby filled with artwork. Rooms are simple, but generally large. Everything is clean, but don't expect new. Not all rooms have air-conditioning. There's no room service, but the staff will be happy to help you order from local restaurants or take your clothes to the cleaners. *Restaurant, bell service, lounge*

Best health club
The Peninsula-New York $$$$
700 Fifth Ave. (at 55th St.)
800 262-9467
241 rooms

The Peninsula Hotel is a place to see. Every room is high-tech with remote controls for lighting, music, TV, and air-conditioning—even in the bathroom! As a matter of fact, the huge marble bathrooms may be the most beautiful in New York City. Wonderful food service and a very helpful concierge desk ("We'll do anything guests ask, as long as it's legal."), and one of the biggest and best spa and health clubs on the roof, make this quite a hotel. *Valet parking, 2 restaurants, lounge, tri-level rooftop health club and spa with heated pool, exercise classes, whirlpool, sauna, and sundeck, 24-hour concierge, business center, 24-hour room service, in-room massage, babysitting, laundry service*

For the budget-minded

The Habitat Hotel $

130 E. 57th St. (at Lexington Ave.)
Built in 1999, offers inexpensive—but small—rooms with style. Near shopping.

The Hotel Newton $

2528 Broadway (between 94th and 95th Sts.)
A nice inexpensive hotel. Large rooms, firm beds, and very clean.

The Lucerne $$

201 W. 79th St. (at Amsterdam Ave.)
Want comfort and service without paying high prices? Large rooms. Great for kids.

Casablanca Hotel $$

147 W. 43rd St.
Free breakfast, coffee, tea, and cookies all day. Free passes to a nearby health club. Small rooms. Unusual Moroccan theme.

C ▸ **PAIR WORK. Use the hotel listings to complete each statement. Explain your answers.**

1. Stella Meyer is 70 years old. She likes to travel, but she has some difficulty with stairs.

   She'd better not stay at _____ _____.

2. Carl Ryan loves to see plays and musicals.

   He should stay at _____ _____.

3. Mark and Nancy Birdsall are traveling with their kids.

   They'd better stay at _____ _____.

4. Lucy Lee loves a hotel that is very comfortable.

   She'd better not stay at _____ _____.

5. Burt and Susan Rey are very active. They run and exercise every day.

   They should stay at _____ _____.

TOP NOTCH
INTERACTION

The best of the best!

STEP 1. **How important are these factors for you in choosing a hotel? Rate these on a scale of 1 to 5. Compare your answers with a partner's.**

not important   very important
◀──────────────────────────▶

price	1 -	2 -	3 -	4 -	5
room size	1 -	2 -	3 -	4 -	5
cleanliness	1 -	2 -	3 -	4 -	5
location	1 -	2 -	3 -	4 -	5
service	1 -	2 -	3 -	4 -	5
amenities	1 -	2 -	3 -	4 -	5
atmosphere	1 -	2 -	3 -	4 -	5

STEP 2. PAIR WORK. Look at all the hotel listings and the map of New York. Choose a hotel. Discuss the advantages and disadvantages of the hotels.

STEP 3. Tell your class about the hotel you chose.

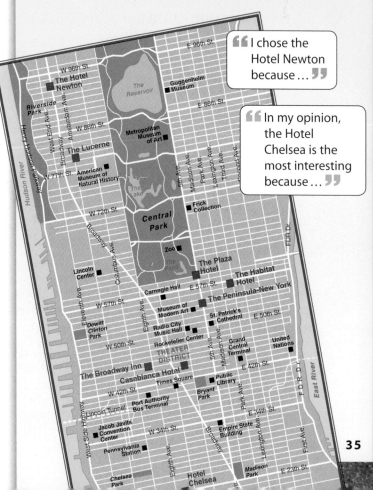

❝I chose the Hotel Newton because …❞

❝In my opinion, the Hotel Chelsea is the most interesting because …❞

A 🎧 **LISTENING COMPREHENSION. Listen carefully to the conversations. Then listen again and check the hotel service or services each person needs.**

	room service	laundry service	shoe shine service	wake-up service	extra hangers	extra towels	make up room
1.	☐	☐	☐	☐	☐	☐	☐
2.	☐	☐	☐	☐	☐	☐	☐
3.	☐	☐	☐	☐	☐	☐	☐
4.	☐	☐	☐	☐	☐	☐	☐

B **What hotel room feature should each guest ask for? Explain your answers.**

1. Ms. Gladstone is traveling alone. She doesn't need much space. _a single room_

2. Mr. and Mrs. Moore are checking into a single room. Their twelve-year-old daughter is with them. _____

3. Donald Lattanzio is very big and tall. He needs a good night's sleep for an important meeting tomorrow. _____

4. Nicole Miller plans to have several meetings with her colleagues. She'd rather not leave the hotel. _____

5. Paul Preston's company wants him to save some money by sharing a room with a colleague. _____

C **Give warnings with _had better_ or _had better not_. Use contractions.**

1. "It's raining. I'm going outside." **YOU** _You'd better take an umbrella_.

2. "It takes Janet 30 minutes to walk to school. Class begins in 15 minutes."
   YOU _____.

3. "My father is arriving at the airport at 6:00. It's almost 5:30 now."
   YOU _____.

4. "We're having an English test tomorrow."
   YOU _____.

5. "I haven't had a vacation in two years."
   YOU _____.

D **WRITING. Choose one of the hotels from the guide on pages 34–35 and write why you would like to stay there. Or write real information about a hotel you have stayed at.**

> Last summer my family and I stayed in a little
> hotel at the beach. The hotel was near the ...

TOP NOTCH **PROJECT**
Where would you like to go for vacation? Use the Internet or a travel guide to find a hotel there. Write the advantages and disadvantages of the hotel.

TOP NOTCH **WEBSITE**
For Unit 3 online activities, visit the *Top Notch* Companion Website at www.longman.com/topnotch.

UNIT WRAP-UP

- **Social language.** Create conversations for the people.
- **Grammar.** Ask questions with <u>will</u> about the picture. Answer the questions.
- **Writing.** Write a description about the hotel for a hotel guide book.

BELL DESK

ROOM 816

RECEPTION

THE BELMAR HOTEL

DIRECTORY

BUSINESS CENTER
9:00 A.M. – 4:00 P.M. 2

GIFT SHOP
9:00 A.M. – 9:00 P.M. Lobby

FITNESS CENTER
6:00 A.M. – 10:00 P.M. 3

SPA
10:00 A.M. – 3:00 P.M. 5

SKYTOP RESTAURANT
8:00 A.M. – 11:00 P.M. 12

✓ *Now I can ...*

☐ leave and take messages.
☐ check in.
☐ request housekeeping services.
☐ choose a hotel.

UNIT 4

Cars and Driving

UNIT GOALS

1 Describe an accident
2 Get service at a service station
3 Rent a car
4 Understand international driving rules

A **TOPIC PREVIEW.** Read the e-mail. Explain what it's for.

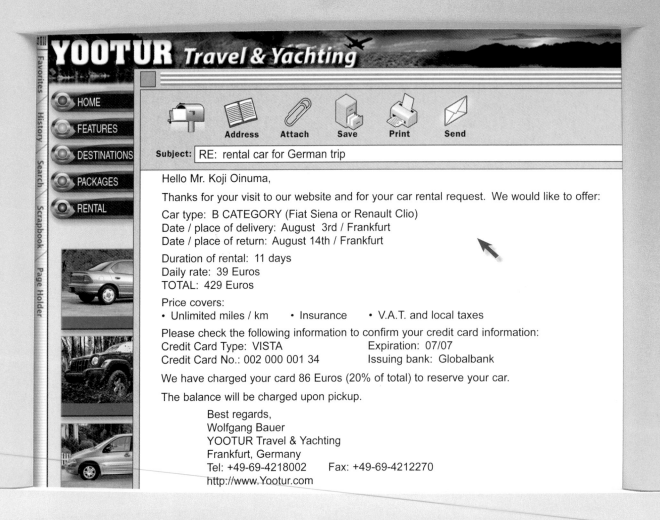

YOOTUR *Travel & Yachting*

Favorites / History / Search / Scrapbook / Page Holder

- HOME
- FEATURES
- DESTINATIONS
- PACKAGES
- RENTAL

Address   Attach   Save   Print   Send

Subject: RE: rental car for German trip

Hello Mr. Koji Oinuma,

Thanks for your visit to our website and for your car rental request. We would like to offer:

Car type: B CATEGORY (Fiat Siena or Renault Clio)
Date / place of delivery: August 3rd / Frankfurt
Date / place of return: August 14th / Frankfurt

Duration of rental: 11 days
Daily rate: 39 Euros
TOTAL: 429 Euros

Price covers:
• Unlimited miles / km   • Insurance   • V.A.T. and local taxes

Please check the following information to confirm your credit card information:
Credit Card Type: VISTA   Expiration: 07/07
Credit Card No.: 002 000 001 34   Issuing bank: Globalbank

We have charged your card 86 Euros (20% of total) to reserve your car.

The balance will be charged upon pickup.

Best regards,
Wolfgang Bauer
YOOTUR Travel & Yachting
Frankfurt, Germany
Tel: +49-69-4218002   Fax: +49-69-4212270
http://www.Yootur.com

B **DISCUSSION.** How long does Mr. Oinuma need the car for? How much will it cost per day? How much does he pay for the reservation?

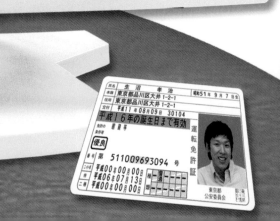

 SOUND BITES. Read along silently as you listen to a conversation in a car rental agency in Germany.

RENTER: Good morning. Koji Oinuma. I have a reservation.
AGENT: Certainly, sir. Just a moment … Oh, yes. We were expecting you. An air-conditioned Clio. Is that with automatic transmission, or manual?
RENTER: Either way.
AGENT: I'll need to see your driver's license and a major credit card.

RENTER: Here you go.
AGENT: I have you returning the car on August 14?
RENTER: That's correct.
AGENT: And will that be here at the airport?
RENTER: Yes. At about 4 p.m. Is that OK?
AGENT: That'll be fine. Here are the keys. The car's right outside.

D Read the conversation again. Check the statements that are true. Explain each response.

- ☐ **1.** The car rental agent knew Mr. Oinuma was coming for a car.
- ☐ **2.** Mr. Oinuma needs to show the agent his passport.
- ☐ **3.** The conversation is in an airport.
- ☐ **4.** Mr. Oinuma will return the car on August 14 in the morning.
- ☐ **5.** Mr. Oinuma pays for the car rental with a credit card.

WHAT ABOUT **YOU?**

Choose a place you'd like to go, a travel date, and a car you'd like to rent. Fill out the online rental request for yourself.

PAIR WORK. Tell your partner where you're going. Did you select the same car?

Sunshine Rentals

Rent-a-Car Booking / Request

Pickup City or Airport:

Return City or Airport:

Car Type:

Pickup Date: (D/M/Y)

Return Date: (D/M/Y)

SEARCH NOW

1 Describe an Accident

MODEL Read and listen.

A: I had an accident.

B: I'm so sorry. Are you OK?

A: I'm fine. No one was hurt.

B: Thank goodness. How did it happen?

A: Well, the other driver was tailgating, and he hit my car.

B: <u>Oh, no!</u> Was there much damage?

A: No. I'll only have to replace a taillight.

∩ **Rhythm and intonation practice**

∩ **Ways to show concern**
Oh, no!
I'm so sorry.
How awful!
I'm sorry to hear that.

A ∩ VOCABULARY. Car parts.
Listen and practice.

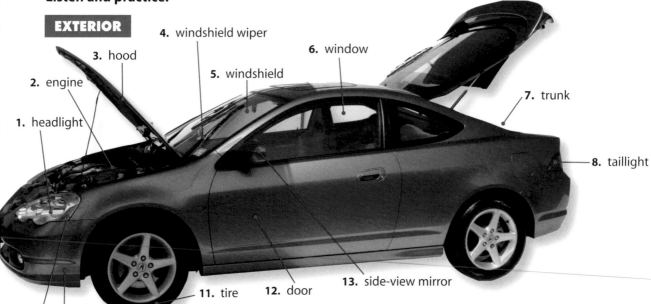

EXTERIOR

4. windshield wiper
6. window
3. hood
5. windshield
2. engine
7. trunk
1. headlight
8. taillight
13. side-view mirror
11. tire
12. door
10. bumper
9. signal

INTERIOR

7. gearshift
8. rearview mirror
9. emergency brake
10. seat belt
1. steering wheel
2. horn
3. dashboard
4. gas pedal
5. clutch
6. brake pedal

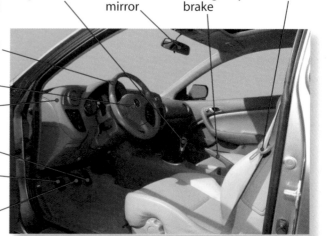

40 UNIT 4

GRAMMAR. The past continuous

Form the past continuous with <u>was</u> or <u>were</u> and a present participle.

What **were** you **doing** last night at eight? I **was watching** TV.

Was the car **making** that noise this morning? Yes, it was. / No, it wasn't.

The past continuous shows an action that continued during a period of time in the past.
The simple past tense shows an action that occurred and then ended.

   past continuous   simple past tense
   I **was going** too fast when I **had** the accident.

GRAMMAR BOOSTER

PAGE G7
For more ...

C   **Complete the paragraph with the past continuous or the simple past tense.**

I _____ an accident on the way to work. I _____ slowly and
     1. have   2. drive

I thought I _____ attention. The problem was that I _____ an
          3. pay   4. wait for

important phone call. When the cell phone _____, I just _____ it.
                                 5. ring   6. answer

All of a sudden, the car in front of me _____, and I _____ it.
                                 7. stop   8. hit

I certainly _____ my lesson. Luckily, I _____ a seat belt when
          9. learn   10. wear

I _____ the accident.
   11. have

D   🎧 **LISTENING COMPREHENSION.** Listen and write the number of the conversation for each picture. Then listen again to check your work.

   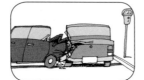    

_____   _____   _____   _____

CONVERSATION
PAIR WORK

**Role-play a conversation about an accident.
Use the pictures or your <u>own</u> ideas.
Start like this:**

A: I had an accident.

B: _____. How did it happen?

A: _____.

B: Was there much damage?

A: _____.

speeding

not paying attention

tailgating

talking on a cell phone

41

CONTROLLED PRACTICE

Get Service at a Service Station

∩ CONVERSATION
MODEL Read and listen.

A: Fill it up, please, with regular.

B: Yes, sir. Anything else?

A: My turn signal isn't working. Can you fix it?

B: Yes, we can. Can you drop the car off tomorrow morning at about 9:00?

A: Sure. What time can I pick it up?

B: How about noon?

A: Terrific. I'll see you at 9:00.

∩ **Rhythm and intonation practice**

∩ **Polite address**

Yes, sir.　　　Yes, ma'am.

A ∩ **VOCABULARY.** Some phrasal verbs. **Listen and practice.**

1. turn on

2. fill up

3. pick up

4. turn off

5. drop off

B Complete each sentence with one of the phrasal verbs.

1. I need gas. Can you please _____?

drop it off / fill it up

2. It's raining, and the windshield wipers are broken. I can't _____.

turn them on / turn them off

3. The car is ready. Can you _____ today at 5:00?

drop it off / pick it up

4. We can do the service on Tuesday. Please _____ early.

drop it off / pick it up

5. What's wrong with these headlights? I can't _____.

fill them up / turn them off

GRAMMAR. Direct object placement with phrasal verbs

Phrasal verbs contain a main verb and a particle (a preposition or adverb) that together have their own meaning.

main verb		particle	
turn	+	on	= start (a machine)

With certain phrasal verbs, direct object nouns can come before or after the particle.

I'll **drop off** the car. OR I'll **drop** the car **off**.

Direct object pronouns, however, must come before the particle.

I'll **drop it off.** (NOT I'll ~~drop off it.~~)

Did you **fill them up?** (NOT Did you ~~fill up them?~~)

Where will they **pick us up?** (NOT Where will they ~~pick up us?~~)

PAGE G8
For more ...

D **PRONUNCIATION.** Stress of particles in phrasal verbs. **Notice the change in stress when an object pronoun comes before the particle. Listen and repeat.**

1. **A:** I'd like to drop off the car.

   B: OK. What time can you drop it off?

2. **A:** They need to pick up the keys.

   B: Great. When do they want to pick them up?

E Unscramble the words to write statements or questions. Then read the sentences aloud.

1. The taillights aren't working. (can't / I / on / them / turn) _____.

2. The car needs service. (off / drop / service station / at / the / I'll / it) _____.

3. It's too cold for air conditioning. (switch / Which / off / it / turns) _____?

4. Thanks for fixing the car. (it / pick / What time / I / can / up) _____?

5. The car is almost out of gas. (up / Please / fill / it) _____.

CONVERSATION
PAIR WORK

Practice asking for service and repairs.
Review the vocabulary on page 40.

A: Fill it up, please, with regular.

B: _____. Anything else?

A: _____. Can you _____?

B: _____ ...

Continue the conversation in your <u>own</u> way.

💡 **Some ideas...**
- won't turn on / turn off
- won't open / close
- (is) making a funny sound
- (is) not working
- (is) stuck

CONTROLLED PRACTICE

43

3 Rent a Car

A 🎧 **VOCABULARY. Types of cars. Listen and practice.**

a sedan

a station wagon

a van

a convertible

an SUV

a sports car

a luxury car

a compact car

a full-size car

B **PAIR WORK. Choose the best kind of car for each person. Discuss your reasons with your partner.**

1 Mr. Taylor is a businessman from Geneva, Switzerland, attending a business meeting in Kota Kinabalu, Malaysia. He doesn't have a lot of luggage. He only needs the car for local travel.

car type: _a compact car_

reason: _He's traveling alone and doesn't need a large car._

2 Ms. Peres is a banker from Porto Alegre, Brazil. Her daughter is getting married in Puebla, Mexico. She wants to drive there from Mexico City with her husband and two other children for the wedding. They have a lot of clothes and presents for the wedding.

car type: _____

reason: _____

3 Mr. Soo is a tourist from Korea, visiting western Australia with his brother. They enjoy hiking and fishing, and they're planning a road trip through the lake district. They plan to drive on some rough roads, so they want a car with four-wheel drive.

car type: _____

reason: _____

4 Ms. Montez is a tourist from Veracruz, Mexico, visiting national parks and cities in the U.S. with her husband and their five children. They plan to do a lot of shopping.

car type: _____

reason: _____

5 Dr. Sato is from Osaka, Japan. He's traveling to an international medical meeting in Buenos Aires, Argentina. He has to invite three doctors to dinner and after-dinner entertainment. He likes to drive.

car type: _____

reason: _____

🎧 **LISTENING COMPREHENSION. Listen to the phone conversations.**

Did the caller rent the car?

| If so, what kind? | [or] | If not, why not? |

1._____ _____

2._____ _____

3._____ _____

4._____ _____

TOP NOTCH
INTERACTION • *Let's rent a car!*

STEP 1. On your notepad, plan a trip for which you need a rental car.

destination	pickup date	drop-off date	number of companions	activities

STEP 2. ROLE PLAY. Choose one or both situations for your trip:

• A telephone call to a car rental agency. Discuss car types, explain your needs, and rent a car for your trip.

• A telephone call to a car rental agency after an accident. Report the accident. Say what you were doing when you had the accident. Discuss repairs.

NEED HELP? **Here's language you already know:**

Offer help
How can I help you?
Certainly, sir / ma'am.
When will you drop off /
    pick up the car?
That'll be fine.

Rent a car
I'd like a [compact car].
I need a car with
    [automatic / manual]
    transmission.

Describe damage
The ____ is / are broken.
The ____ is / are not working.
The ____ won't open / close /
    turn on / turn off.
The ____ is stuck.

Express concern
How did it happen?
Oh, no!
How awful!
I'm so sorry.
I'm sorry to hear that.
Thank goodness!

Discuss the accident
Was there much damage?
I / The other driver was
    [speeding].
I hit another car.
Another car hit me.
No one was hurt.

4 Understand International Driving Rules

A **READING WARM-UP.** Are you a good driver? If you don't drive a car, would you like to learn?

B 🎧 **READING.** Read the article about driving a car abroad. Do you think this information is important?

TIPS ON DRIVING ABROAD

It can be difficult to drive in another country. First, driving rules and laws differ from country to country. So do road signs. And, people in different countries drive on opposite sides of the road! Here are some tips on driving abroad.

First, obtain an International Driving Permit (IDP). Most countries accept this permit. It's easy to get an IDP. Just enter "International Driving Permit" in any Internet search engine and you will get the information you need.

Once you have the IDP, carry your own driver's license with you any time you drive outside your own country.

If possible, get a copy of the foreign country's rules before you begin driving in that country. An excellent source of information is a car rental company in the foreign country.

Be aware:
- Some countries have a minimum and maximum driving age.
- Some countries have penalties for drivers and/or passengers who don't wear a seat belt. Always "buckle up."
- Many countries require you to honk your horn before going around a sharp corner or to flash your lights before passing.
- If the drivers in the country you are visiting drive on the opposite side of the road from your own country, it may be a good idea to practice driving in a quiet area before attempting to drive in heavy traffic.

And a word about road signs: In general, the color red on an international road sign signals negative information, such as a warning or prohibition, whereas blue is positive. Simply put, blue says *do*, red says *don't*.

SOURCE: http://travel.state.gov

See how many international road signs you know.

2 SLIPPERY ROAD	
☐ MINIMUM SPEED	1
☐ MAXIMUM SPEED [SPEED LIMIT]	
☐ NO PASSING	2
☐ DANGER	
☐ PEDESTRIAN CROSSING	3
☐ NO ENTRY	
☐ PARKING AREA	4
☐ NO STOPPING	
☐ NO PARKING	5

🚫 (50) (30) P   6

10 **9** **8** **7**

Answers: 1. NO ENTRY 2. SLIPPERY ROAD 3. PEDESTRIAN CROSSING 4. DANGER 5. NO PASSING 6. NO STOPPING 7. PARKING AREA 8. MINIMUM SPEED 9. MAXIMUM SPEED 10. NO PARKING

SOURCE: http://www.ideamerge.com

C **Check all the statements that are true, according to the article. Explain your responses.**

☐ **1.** It's difficult to get an international driving permit to drive in another country.

☐ **2.** You should always carry your driver's license when you drive in another country.

☐ **3.** Foreign car rental companies can tell you local driving rules.

☐ **4.** It's never necessary to wear a seat belt outside of your own country.

☐ **5.** The color of a road sign can help you understand what it means.

D **DISCUSSION.** Discuss the difficulties of driving abroad. What should you do before the trip?

INTERACTION • *What makes a good driver?*

STEP 1. PAIR WORK. With your partner, complete the survey about bad driving practices. (If you don't drive, answer the questions about someone you know.)

Do you ...

☐ speed?

☐ tailgate?

☐ honk your horn unnecessarily?

☐ cut off other drivers?

☐ talk on a cell phone when you drive?

☐ not pay attention?

☐ not stop at stop signs?

☐ not signal?

☐ flash your lights at other drivers?

☐ weave through traffic?

Score one point for each check.

	POINTS	0–1	2–4	5–7	8–10
ACCIDENT PROBABILITY		ALMOST 0%			100%

STEP 2. PAIR WORK. Discuss do's and don'ts for drivers. Make a list on your notepad. Compare your list with other classmates' lists.

do:	don't:
buckle up	tailgate

STEP 3. WRITING. On a separate sheet of paper, write about good drivers and bad drivers. Use your notepad and the survey for support.

Good drivers know the driving rules and laws. They always stop...

FREE PRACTICE

UNIT 4
CHECKPOINT

A 🎧 **LISTENING COMPREHENSION.** Listen carefully to the people renting cars. Write the number of the conversation below the kind of car they want.

____   ____   ____   ____   ____   ____

B **Choose a response to each statement or question.**

1. "Was there any damage?"
   a. Yes. He was tailgating.   **b.** Yes. The taillights are broken.

2. "Fill it up, please."
   a. Sure. What time can I pick it up?   **b.** Sure. Anything else?

3. "No one was hurt."
   a. I'm so sorry to hear that.   **b.** Thank goodness.

4. "I was talking on my cell phone, and I hit another car."
   a. Oh, no!   **b.** Was he speeding?

C **Complete each statement about cars.**

1. A small, fast car is a _____sports car_____.

2. When you drive too fast, you are _____.

3. The light that indicates the direction you want to turn is the _____.

4. The lights on the front of the car are the _____.

5. If you want to check the engine, you have to open the _____.

6. When you want to stop or slow the car, step on the _____.

D **Complete each statement or question with the past continuous or the simple past tense.**

1. I _____, and I _____ an accident.
   _{speed} ... _{have}

2. The other driver _____ a seat belt, and
   _{not wear}
   she _____ at the stop sign.
   _{not stop}

3. She _____ on a cell phone and _____.
   _{talk} ... _{not pay attention}

4. Who _____ when the accident _____?
   _{drive} ... _{happen}

5. Where _____ they _____ when the
   _{go}
   phone _____?
   _{ring}

> 🎧 **TOP NOTCH SONG**
> "Wheels Around the World"
> Lyrics on last page before Workbook.

>
> **TOP NOTCH PROJECT**
> Research car accidents in your local newspaper or on the Internet. Describe an accident to your class.

>
> **TOP NOTCH WEBSITE**
> For Unit 4 online activities, visit the *Top Notch* Companion Website at www.longman.com/topnotch.

UNIT WRAP-UP

- **Narration.** Tell a story, using the pictures.
- **Social language.** Create conversations for the people.
- **Writing.** Describe the accident and its causes.

MULTI CAR RENTALS

January 16

Pucon, Chile

JANUARY 16 ARRIVAL 14:45

January 17

January 18

MULTI CAR RENTALS

Later

Now I can ...

- ☐ describe an accident.
- ☐ get service at a service station.
- ☐ rent a car.
- ☐ understand international driving rules.

49

Personal Care and Appearance

UNIT GOALS

1 Ask for something you can't find
2 Request salon services
3 Schedule and pay for personal care
4 Discuss ways to improve appearance

A ▶ **TOPIC PREVIEW.** Which of these products do you buy regularly? Where do you buy them: in a drugstore, a cosmetics store, online, or someplace else?

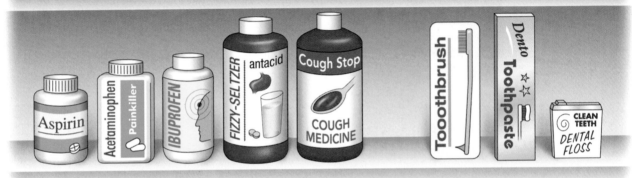

B ▶ **PAIR WORK.** With your partner, classify the products and write them in the chart.

Hair care	Tooth care	Skin care	Shaving	Makeup	Medicine
shampoo					

 C 🎧 **SOUND BITES.** Read along silently as you listen to a conversation at a meeting in Brazil.

MIEKO: Hey, Noor. I need to pick up a few things on the way back to the hotel. Feel like stopping at a cosmetics store? We could get some of that makeup these gorgeous Brazilians wear.

NOOR: I'd like to, but I think I'll pass. I don't have much time today. I'm expecting an important call from Kuala Lumpur in a few minutes.

MIEKO: No problem. I'll just go myself. But wish me luck. I'm sure no one speaks Japanese!

NOOR: Don't worry. Most people speak some English. You'll be fine.

MIEKO: I guess. In any case, the store's self-service. It'll be a piece of cake!

NOOR: See you back at the hotel.

D Read the conversation again. **Correct the following false statements.**

1. Mieko is going to shop in a store in the hotel.
2. Noor can't go with Mieko because she has to call Kuala Lumpur.
3. Noor is worried that no one speaks Japanese.

E **UNDERSTANDING MEANING FROM CONTEXT.** Complete each statement, according to the conversations.

1. When Noor says, "I think I'll pass," she means _____.
2. When Noor says, "You'll be fine," she means _____.
3. When Mieko says, "It'll be a piece of cake," she means _____.

WHAT ABOUT **YOU?**

Complete the chart about the things **you** buy and your reasons.

Product	What brand?	Reason
shampoo		
soap		
toothpaste		

DISCUSSION. On the board, write a list of all the shampoo, soap, and toothpaste brands your classmates use. Do you all agree on which brands are the best?

1 *Ask for Something You Can't Find*

🎧 CONVERSATION MODEL Read and listen.

A: Excuse me. Where would I find toothpaste?

B: Toothpaste? Have a look in aisle two.

A: Actually, I did and there wasn't any.

B: I'm sorry. Let me get you some from the back.

A: Thanks so much.

🎧 **Rhythm and intonation practice**

A 🎧 **VOCABULARY.** Personal care products. **Listen and practice.**

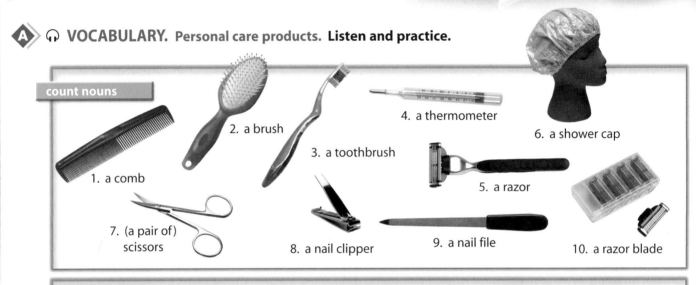

count nouns

1. a comb
2. a brush
3. a toothbrush
4. a thermometer
5. a razor
6. a shower cap
7. (a pair of) scissors
8. a nail clipper
9. a nail file
10. a razor blade

non-count nouns

1. soap
2. deodorant
3. toothpaste
4. hair spray
5. sunscreen
6. dental floss
7. makeup
8. shampoo
9. shaving cream
10. body lotion

B 🎧 **LISTENING COMPREHENSION.** **Listen carefully to the ads for personal care products. Choose the kind of product it is. Then listen again and check your work.**

1. Spring Rain	☐ shampoo	☐ deodorant
2. Rose	☐ soap	☐ conditioner
3. Pro-Tect	☐ hand cream	☐ sunscreen
4. All Over	☐ body lotion	☐ soap
5. Scrubbie	☐ toothpaste	☐ shaving cream

C ▷ GRAMMAR. Count and non-count nouns: indefinite quantities and amounts

Some and any

Use <u>some</u> and <u>any</u> with both count and non-count nouns.

Use <u>some</u> in affirmative statements.

We bought **some** nail files. Now we have **some**.

They need **some** soap. We have **some**.

Use <u>any</u> in negative statements.

I don't have **any** razors, and I don't want **any**.

We don't want **any** deodorant. We don't need **any**.

Use <u>some</u> or <u>any</u> in questions.

Do you want **some** shampoo? OR Do you want **any** shampoo?

A lot of, many, and much

Use <u>a lot of</u> with both count and non-count nouns in statements and questions.

That store has **a lot of** razors. They don't have **a lot of** nail files. Do they have **a lot of** lotion?

Use <u>many</u> and <u>much</u> in negative statements.

Use <u>many</u> with count nouns.

They don't have **many** brands of makeup.

Use <u>much</u> with non-count nouns.

The store doesn't have **much** toothpaste.

GRAMMAR BOOSTER

PAGES G8–G9
For more …

D ▷ Complete the conversation between a husband and a wife getting ready for a family trip.

DANA: Do we have _____ shampoo?

    1. any / many

NEIL: Yes. We have _____ shampoo.

    2. many / a lot of

DANA: And Maggie uses _____ conditioner. Is there _____?

    3. much / a lot of   4. many / any

NEIL: No. There isn't _____ conditioner. And we don't have _____

    5. some / any   6. much / many

toothpaste, either. I can pick _____ up on my way home.

    7. some / any

DANA: Hey, Adam's shaving now. Does he need _____ razor blades?

    8. any / much

What about _____ aftershave lotion?

    9. some / many

NEIL: He doesn't shave every day. He can use mine.

CONVERSATION PAIR WORK

Role-play shopping for personal care products. Use the directory.

A: Excuse me. Where would I find _____?

B: _____? Have a look in aisle _____.

A: Actually, _____.

B: _____ …

Continue the conversation. Ask about other personal care products.

Cosmetics Plus Directory	
	AISLE
Hair Care	3
Tooth Care	4
Skin Care	2
Nail Care	2
Makeup	2
Cold and Flu Medicine	1
Shaving Supplies	1

CONTROLLED PRACTICE

2 ▸ *Request Salon Services*

🎧 CONVERSATION
MODEL Read and listen.

A: I'm Linda Court. I have a two o'clock appointment for a haircut with Sean.

B: Hello, Ms. Court. Sean's running a little late. Can I get you some coffee or tea?

A: No, thanks. Can I get a manicure in the meantime?

B: Yes, but it'll be a few minutes. There's someone ahead of you.

🎧 **Rhythm and intonation practice**

A 🎧 **VOCABULARY.** Salon services. **Listen and practice.**

1. a shampoo

2. a shave

3. a haircut

B **GRAMMAR.** <u>Someone</u> / <u>anyone</u>

Use <u>someone</u> in affirmative statements.
There's **someone** ahead of you.

Use <u>anyone</u> in negative statements.
There isn't **anyone** waiting.

Use <u>someone</u> or <u>anyone</u> in questions.
Can **someone** wash my hair?
Can **anyone** give me a manicure?

GRAMMAR BOOSTER

PAGE G10
For more ...

4. a manicure

5. a pedicure

C **Complete each statement or question with <u>someone</u> or <u>anyone</u>.**

1. There's _____ at the front desk.

2. They didn't tell _____ that it would be a long wait.

3. Did you see _____ giving a manicure?

4. I don't have the scissors. I gave them to _____.

5. There will be _____ here to give you a pedicure in a few minutes, if you can wait.

6. Please don't tell _____ the price. It was very expensive!

7. Did you tell _____ how long you've been waiting?

8. _____ called and left you this message while you were getting your shampoo.

9. Please give this list of services to _____ to check.

10. There wasn't _____ there when she called for an appointment.

11. _____ told me to wait a few minutes.

12. I didn't ask _____ about the price.

D 🎧 **LISTENING COMPREHENSION.** Listen carefully to the conversations. Check the service(s) each client wants.

1.	☐	☐	☐	☐	☐
2.	☐	☐	☐	☐	☐
3.	☐	☐	☐	☐	☐
4.	☐	☐	☐	☐	☐

E 🎧 **PRONUNCIATION.** Vowel reduction to /ə/. The vowel in an unstressed syllable is often reduced to /ə/. Listen and repeat.

1. ma ni cure
   /ə/
2. pe di cure
   /ə/
3. me di cine
   /ə/
4. de o do rant
   /ə/

CONVERSATION
PAIR WORK

Role-play requesting salon services. Use the list. Start like this:

A: I'm _____. I have _____ appointment for a _____ with _____.

B: Hello, _____. _____'s running a little late. Can I get you some _____?

A: _____ …

Continue the role play in your own way.

UNISEX SALON
Services   Staff

shampoo   *Lisa / Olga*

haircut   *Judy / Christopher / Bruce*

manicure   *Sonia / Natasha*

pedicure   *Karin*

shave   *Nick*

Schedule and Pay for Personal Care

A 🎧 **VOCABULARY.** Schedule and pay for personal care.
Listen and practice.

Would it be possible to get a facial?
I don't have an appointment.

How long will I have to wait?

How much do you charge
for a massage?

Is it customary to leave a tip?

Can I charge it to my room?

I'm sorry. I have to cancel
my appointment.

B Complete each conversation. Use the expressions from the vocabulary and
your <u>own</u> ideas.

1. **A:** _____?
   B: Let me check the price list.

2. **A:** _____?
   B: Well, you're in luck. A customer just canceled his appointment.

3. **A:** _____?
   B: Certainly. What's your room number?

4. **A:** _____?
   B: About 35 minutes. Is that OK?

5. **A:** _____?
   B: Yes, it is. Most people give about 10 percent.

C 🎧 **LISTENING COMPREHENSION.** Listen to the conversations in a salon.
Check what each client asks about. Then listen again and explain to a partner
what happened.

1. **a.** ☐ getting a massage   **b.** ☐ getting a manicure

2. **a.** ☐ waiting for a manicure   **b.** ☐ paying for a manicure

3. **a.** ☐ getting a haircut   **b.** ☐ charging a haircut to her room

4. **a.** ☐ tipping someone   **b.** ☐ getting a shampoo

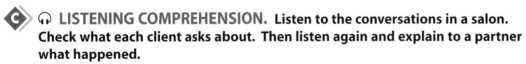

INTERACTION • *Pamper yourself!*

ROLE PLAY. Look at the date book of the Finis Terra Hotel. Role-play conversations to request services, schedule appointments, and ask about payment.

Finis Terra
HOTEL & SPA

SATURDAY, JULY 10 192/174

	Spa facial	Deluxe manicure	Full massage	Neck and shoulder massage	Pedicure and foot massage
	Katya	Lucille	Tom	Kevin	May
				Ms. Cruz	
9 00	Mr. Santos				
9 15					
9 30					Mr. Loyola
9 45	Ms. Pleva	Mr. Drucker			
10 00					
10 15					
10 30			Mr. Yu		
10 45	Ms. Kumar				
11 00					Ms. Joon
11 15					
11 30					
11 45		Ms. Gomez			
12 00					
12 15				Ms. Benson	
12 30					
12 45	Mr. Dialo				
1 00					
1 15					
1 30					
1 45					
2 00					
2 15					
2 30					
2					
3					
3					
3					
3					
4					
4					
4					
4					
5 00					
5 15					
5 30					

NEED HELP? Here's language you already know:

Payment
How much do you charge for a ____?
Can I charge it to my room?
Is it customary to leave a tip?

Client
Can I get a ____?
Would it be possible to get a ____?
How long will I have to wait?
Can I get a ____ in the meantime?
I'm ____. I have ____ appointment for a ____ with ____.

Salon's Staff
It'll be a few minutes.
There's someone ahead of you.
You're in luck.
[She's] running a little late.
Can I get you [some tea]?

JULY 11 193/173

Discuss Ways to Improve Appearance

A ▶ **READING WARM-UP.** What are some things people can do to improve their appearance?

B ▶ 🎧 **READING.** Read the magazine article about cosmetic surgery. Do you think people should consider these solutions to their problems?

Cosmetic surgery—Q&A for everyone?

Cosmetic surgeons have made great progress in restoring normal appearance by repairing injuries and removing scars from burns and other injuries. More and more, however, many people with the necessary financial resources have chosen cosmetic surgery—an expensive option—to improve their appearance. Gail Weiss, *Fitness and Health Magazine*'s medical editor, answers readers' questions about cosmetic surgery.

BEFORE cosmetic surgery **AFTER** cosmetic surgery

Dear Dr. Weiss:
When I was young, I was a chocoholic. I ate a lot of chocolate, but I never gained any weight. Now that I'm older, I can't eat anything without gaining weight! I've heard that liposuction is the answer to an overweight person's dreams. What's up with that?
                                    Dawson

Dear Dawson:
It's true that liposuction can remove fat deposits that don't respond to dieting and exercise, but it's expensive and can be dangerous. It would be a good idea to ask your doctor for some help in dieting first. Then, if you are unsuccessful, be sure to find a surgeon with a lot of experience before deciding on liposuction.
                          Gail Weiss, M.D.

Dear Dr. Weiss:
I'm a 24-year-old man who is already losing his hair! Dr. Weiss, I'm looking for a wife and I'm afraid no woman will want to marry a 25-year-old baldie! I need some advice.
                                    Calvin

Dear Calvin:
There are several surgical procedures which a cosmetic surgeon can perform to help treat hair loss and restore hair for both men and women. But if that's not practical, remember that some of the world's most attractive men are bald!
                          Gail Weiss, M.D.

Dear Dr. Weiss:
Can anyone help me with my problem? I have too much hair on my body and I'm sick and tired of shaving. It's so embarrassing.
                                    Cassandra

Dear Cassandra:
Before you call a cosmetic surgeon for hair removal, try a depilatory cream. Depilatories are available in any drugstore and they remove hair easily and safely in your own home. Why don't you give that a try first?
                          Gail Weiss, M.D.

Dear Dr. Weiss:
I'm at my wits' end with my face. I have wrinkles and sun damage. I'm only 30, but I look 50. Do you think a face-lift is an option for me?
                                    Josephine

Dear Josephine:
Both men and women of all ages request this popular and effective surgery. It lifts the face and the neck in one operation and has excellent results. But this is surgery, and afterwards you will have to stay at home for a number of days. It takes time to recover. And you may have to do it again after a number of years. Before you decide to have a face-lift, ask your dermatologist or a cosmetic surgeon about a chemical peel. A chemical peel removes the top layer of skin and can improve the appearance of the skin without surgery. Good luck!
                          Gail Weiss, M.D.

INFORMATION SOURCE:
American Academy of Cosmetic Surgery
http://www.cosmeticsurgery.org

C **PAIR WORK.** Complete the chart with information from the article. Explain your answers.

	Problem	Dr. Weiss's advice
Dawson	*overweight*	*diet first*
Calvin		
Cassandra		
Josephine		

TOP NOTCH
INTERACTION • *Would you ever get a face-lift?*

STEP 1. Take the personal opinion survey about ways to improve appearance.

Would you try...?

	definitely	maybe	probably not	absolutely not!
diet	○	○	○	○
exercise	○	○	○	○
massage	○	○	○	○
creams and lotions	○	○	○	○
hair removal	○	○	○	○
hair restoration	○	○	○	○
makeup	○	○	○	○
facials	○	○	○	○
face-lifts	○	○	○	○
liposuction	○	○	○	○
chemical peels	○	○	○	○

STEP 2. PAIR WORK. Choose one method you would try and one method you would not try. On the notepad, write advantages and disadvantages. Compare your notepad with a partner's.

method	advantage(s)	disadvantage(s)
I would try diet.	free, safe	hard to do!

STEP 3. DISCUSSION. What's the best way to improve appearance?

STEP 4. WRITING. Write a letter to Dr. Weiss. Then exchange letters with your partner and write a response.

CHECKPOINT

A 🎧 **LISTENING COMPREHENSION. Listen carefully to the conversations. Complete the statements.**

1. Hawaii Bronzer is a brand of _____.
2. Swan is a brand of _____.
3. Truly You is a brand of _____.
4. Mountain Fresh is a brand of _____.
5. Silk 'n' Satin is a brand of _____.

B **Give advice to each person.**

1. "My nails are a mess!"

YOU _You should get a manicure_____.

2. "Just look at my hair! What should I do?"

YOU _____.

3. "Oh, my aching back! I played tennis and then I cleaned the house."

YOU _____.

C **Complete each statement or question.**

1. There aren't _____ customers in the store right now.

many / much
2. Do they have _____ good shampoo at the spa?

any / many
3. Your sister doesn't want _____ conditioner.

some / any
4. You don't have _____ makeup in the bathroom.

much / some
5. My son uses _____ razor blades.

any / a lot of
6. It's not good to give children _____ cough medicine.

some / a lot of

D **Choose a response to each question.**

1. "Facials are two for the price of one. Feel like getting a facial with me?"
   a. It's not customary to tip.   **b.** I think I'll pass.

2. "Can I get a manicure in the meantime?"
   a. Actually, we don't have many.   **b.** Certainly. Right over there.

3. "How much do you charge for a shave and a haircut?"
   a. You can charge it to your room.   **b.** I'm not sure. Let me check.

E **WRITING. On a separate sheet of paper, write about a personal care product you like. What does it do for you? Why do you buy it?**

> I've used Scrubbie Toothpaste since I was a child. First of all, it tastes great. It's also a very popular ...

TOP NOTCH **PROJECT**
Bring in ads for cosmetics and makeup. What do the ads say they can do to improve appearance? Make a bulletin board of products.

TOP NOTCH **WEBSITE**
For Unit 5 online activites, visit the *Top Notch* Companion Website at www.longman.com/topnotch.

Medicine	1	Hair Care	3
Makeup	2	Shaving	3
Nail Care	2	Skin Care	4
Tooth Care	2		

UNIT WRAP-UP

- **Vocabulary.** Name the personal care products you see. Make a list of other products you think you can find in the store.

- **Grammar.** Make statements with <u>some</u>, <u>any</u>, <u>many</u>, <u>much</u>, and <u>a lot of</u>.

  There's a lot of makeup in the store.

- **Social language.** Go shopping. Ask the clerk for products.

Aisle 2

Aisle 3

✔ **Now I can ...**

- ☐ ask for something I can't find.
- ☐ request salon services.
- ☐ schedule and pay for personal care.
- ☐ discuss ways to improve appearance.

61

This is an alphabetical list of all productive vocabulary in the *Top Notch 2* units. The numbers refer to the page on which the word first appears or is defined. When a word has two meanings, both are in the list. Entries for 2A are in black. Entries for 2B are in blue.

A

a lot of   53
accident   40
action film   18
addict   66
address people   2
afraid of   78
agree   23
air-conditioned   39
airport shuttle   27
aisle   52
allergic to   64
almost   100
already   7
always   16
angry about   78
animated film   18
any   53
anyone   54
apologize for   78
appointment   54
art exhibition   5
as   100
asparagus   65
automatic transmission   39
avoid   64

B

babysitting   27
before   7
believe in   78
bell service   27
birth order   82
blue   75
body lotion   52
bored with   78
boring   20
bow   2
bowl   90
brake   40
brand   51
bring up (a newspaper)   32
brush   52
bumper   40
business card   2
business center   31

C

calm   77
can't stand   66

CD drive   98
cell phone   118
charge   115
charming   82
cheer (someone) up   75
cheerful   77
chewy   70
chocolate   65
clay   90
click on (an icon)   102
climb   6
cloth   90
clown   82
clutch   40
comb   52
comedy   18
compact car   44
complain about   78
convertible   44
cool   90
copy text   102
cosmetic surgery   58
crash   102
crazy about   66
create a web page   104
creative   82
crunchy   70
cut off other drivers   47
cut text   102

D

damage   40
dashboard   40
definitely   66
dental floss   52
dentures (a set of)   118
deodorant   52
depressing   77
diamond ring   118
disagree   23
disgusting   77
documentary   18
don't agree with me   64
don't care for   64
door (car)   40
double room   30
double standard   116
down   75
down in the dumps   75

download   99
drama   18
drawing   87
driver's license   39
drop off   42

E

emergency brake   40
emotions   80
engine   40
environment   80
ever   7
exchange   2
excited about   78
exciting   77
extra   32
extrovert   81
eyeglasses (a pair of)   118

F

facial   56
familiar   4
fantastic   90
fascinated by   94
fashion   87
feel   23
figure   90
fill up   42
film   87
fitness center   31
flash lights   47
for   16
fries   65
full-size car   44
funny   20

G

game   98
gas pedal   40
gearshift   40
genetics   80
gesture   8
get stuck in traffic   17
gift shop   31
glass   90
go sightseeing   6
go to the top of   6
gold   90
gorgeous   90

greetings   2
gym   5

H

had better   31
hair care   50
hair spray   52
hair dryer   32
haircut   54
hanger   32
happy   77
happy about   78
hard   70
headlight   40
headset   98
hers   112
his   112
honk   47
hood   40
horn   40
horror film   18
hug   2

I

ice cream   65
icon   102
influenced by   94
inspired by   94
instant message   99
interested in   94
Internet connection   27
introvert   81
iron   32

J

join a chat room   104
joystick   98
just   16

K

keyboard   98
king-size bed   30
kiss   2

L

last name   2
late   16
lately   16
laundry   27
lifestyle   65
look (like)   70

Social language list for 2A and 2B

This is a unit-by-unit list of all the productive social language from *Top Notch 2*.

Unit 1

You look familiar.
Have we met before?
I don't think so.
I'm not from around here.
As a matter of fact, I am.
Oh, that's right! Now I remember.

What have you been up to?
Not much.
[Audrey], have you met [Hanah]?
[Hanah], I'd like you to meet [Audrey].
I think we've met before.
Good to see you again.

Welcome to [Rio].
Have you ever been here before?
No. It's my first time.
Have you tried [feijoada] yet?
I think you'll like it.

Unit 2

You're going to love [this theater].
I'm really in the mood for [a good classic movie].
I missed it.
They say it's [great].
Actually, I'd rather see something else.
Deal!
Sorry I'm late. Have you been here long?
For about [10] minutes. Not too bad.
I got stuck in traffic.
I missed the bus.

I couldn't get a taxi.
I couldn't find a parking space.
The [8:00] show for [The Train] is sold out.
How much do I owe?
Nothing. It's on me.
Next time it's my treat.
I've always wanted to see [Hitchcock's The Birds].
What would you rather see—a [comedy] or a [musical]?
It doesn't matter to me.

What do you think of [Madonna]?
Actually, not much.
For real? (to express surprise)
That's what makes the world go 'round!
Who was in it?
What was it about?
What kind of movie was it?
Was it good?
Do you recommend it?
I agree / disagree.

Unit 3

I'm checking out.
Was your stay satisfactory?
Will you be putting this on your [Vista card]?
Thank you for staying with us.
I'd like to speak to [Anne Smith].
I'll ring that room for you.

He's / She's not answering.
Would you like to leave a message?
Please tell him [Tim Klein] called.
Please tell her I'll call back later.
Please tell him I'll be [at the Clayton Hotel] until [5:00].
Please tell her I'll be at [22-56-838]
Is that all?

I'm checking in. The name's [Smith].
How do you want to pay?
By the way, is the [restaurant] still open?
Actually, you'd better hurry.

Unit 4

I have a reservation.
We were expecting you.
I'll need to see your [driver's license and a major credit card].
That's correct.
That'll be fine.
I had an accident.
How awful.
Oh no!
I'm sorry to hear that.
I'm so sorry. Are you OK?
No one was hurt.

Thank goodness. How did it happen?
[The other driver] was [speeding].
I hit another car. / Another car hit me.
Was there much damage?
I'll only have to replace [a taillight].
Fill it up, please, with [regular].
Yes, sir / ma'am.
Anything else?
My [turn signal] isn't working. Can you fix it?
Can you drop the car off [tomorrow morning] at about [9:00]?

What time can I pick it up?
How's [noon]?
Terrific. I'll see you at [9:00].
[My headlight] won't turn on / turn off.
[My car trunk] won't open / close.
[My engine] is making a funny sound.
[My headlight] isn't working.
[My car window] is stuck.

Unit 5

I need to pick up a few things on the way back to [the hotel].
Feel like stopping at [a cosmetics store] with me?
I'd like to, but I think I'll pass.
I don't have much time today.
It'll be a piece of cake.
Where would I find [toothpaste]?
Have a look in [aisle 2].

Actually, I did and there wasn't any.
Let me get you some from the back.
I have [a two o'clock] appointment for a [haircut] with [Sean].
[Sean] is running a little late.
Can I get you some [coffee] or [tea]?
Can I get a [manicure] in the meantime?
Yes, but it'll be a few minutes.
There's someone ahead of you.

Would it be possible to get a [facial]?
I don't have an appointment.
How long will I have to wait?
How much do you charge for a [massage]?
Is it customary to leave a tip?
Can I charge it to my room?
I'm sorry. I have to cancel my appointment.

Unit 6

What in the world are you [eating]?
I used to be. Not anymore.
To tell you the truth, it was just too much trouble.
Want to try some?
You only live once.
Everything's ready. Why don't we [sit down]?
This [food] looks great!
It really smells delicious.
Please help yourself.

Thanks. But I'll pass on the [chicken].
Don't you eat [chicken]?
I'm on a diet.
I'm trying to lose weight.
I'm avoiding [sugar].
I'm a vegetarian.
I'm allergic to [chocolate].
[Coffee] doesn't agree with me.
I'm sorry. I didn't know that.
Don't worry about it. It's not a problem.

I used to have it a lot. But I've been cutting back.
I couldn't live without it.
I'm [not] crazy about [seafood].
I'm a big [meat] eater / [coffee] drinker.
I'm a [chocolate] addict / [pizza] lover.
I can't stand [fish].
I don't care for [steak].
I'm not much of a [pizza] eater / [coffee] lover.

Unit 7

What do you feel like doing after dinner?
I'm kind of down in the dumps.
You (do) look a little blue. Something wrong?
Nothing I can put my finger on.
I guess I'm just feeling a little out of sorts.

Maybe [a nice dinner] will cheer you up.
Why don't we [go for a walk]?
Would you like me to [make you some soup]?
How about some [ice cream]? That always makes me feel better.
How about [gray]? (to talk about color preference)

[Gray]'s out of the question.
What's wrong with [gray]?
You look down. What's up?
Oh, nothing serious.
I'm just tired of the same old grind.
But thanks for asking.
I know what you mean.

Unit 8

This [print]'s sort of interesting.
I kind of like it.
It would look nice [over my desk].
Don't you find it a little too [dark]?
I guess I'm not really into [bright colors].
To each his own.
Be sure not to miss [the Prado Museum] while you're in [Madrid].
Really? Why's that?

Well, for one thing, [Las Meninas] is [kept] there.
No kidding! I've always wanted to see that.
Thanks for the suggestion.
What's this [figure] made of?
Wood. It's handmade.
What is it used for?
When were they made?

How were they made?
What do you think of it?
I'm not crazy about it / them.
I don't care for it / them.
It's not for me.
They're fantastic / gorgeous / wonderful / cool.

Unit 9

Am I interrupting you?
[I'm] just fooling around.
What are you up to?
I logged on to [send you some pictures].
Cool!
[I] can't wait to [download them].

I'm thinking about getting [a new monitor].
Oh, yeah? What kind?
Everyone says I should get [a Macro].
Well, I've heard that the [Panatel] is as [good] as the [Macro].

Really? I'll check it out.
[Eugene], could you take a look at this?
Sure. What's the problem?
Why don't you try [restarting]?
OK. I'll give that a try.

Unit 10

Your parents would let you do that?
Are you kidding?
I'd have to be nuts to [ask them].
There's nothing wrong with [tattoos]. Everybody has [them].
I hate to say this, but I think you're making a mistake.
You should get permission. If you don't, I'm sure you'll be sorry.

I'll give it some thought.
Excuse me, I think you forgot something.
My pleasure.
You're welcome.
Don't mention it.
Not at all.
Sure. (to acknowledge thanks)
They didn't charge us for the [desserts].

They undercharged me.
They gave me too much change.
They gave me more than I ordered.
You think so?
Absolutely.
Definitely.
Of course.
Sure. (to express certainty)

Pronunciation table

These are the pronunciation symbols used in *Top Notch 2*.

Vowels

Symbol	Key Word	Symbol	Key Word
i	beat, feed	ə	banana, among
ɪ	bit, did	ɚ	shirt, murder
eɪ	date, paid	aɪ	bite, cry, buy, eye
ɛ	bet, bed	aʊ	about, how
æ	bat, bad	ɔɪ	voice, boy
ɑ	box, odd, father	ɪr	deer
ɔ	bought, dog	ɛr	bare
oʊ	boat, road	ɑr	bar
ʊ	book, good	ɔr	door
u	boot, food, flu	ʊr	tour
ʌ	but, mud, mother		

Consonants

Symbol	Key Word	Symbol	Key Word
p	pack, happy	z	zip, please, goes
b	back, rubber	ʃ	ship, machine, station, special, discussion
t	tie		
d	die		
k	came, key, quick	ʒ	measure, vision
g	game, guest	h	hot, who
tʃ	church, nature, watch	m	men
dʒ	judge, general, major	n	sun, know, pneumonia
f	fan, photograph	ŋ	sung, ringing
v	van	w	wet, white
θ	thing, breath	l	light, long
ð	then, breathe	r	right, wrong
s	sip, city, psychology	y	yes
		t̪	butter, bottle
		t˺	button

Irregular verbs

base form	simple past	past participle	base form	simple past	past participle
be	was / were	been	leave	left	left
become	became	become	let	let	let
begin	began	begun	lose	lost	lost
break	broke	broken	make	made	made
bring	brought	brought	mean	meant	meant
build	built	built	meet	met	met
buy	bought	bought	pay	paid	paid
catch	caught	caught	put	put	put
choose	chose	chosen	quit	quit	quit
come	came	come	read /rid/	read /rɛd/	read /rɛd/
cost	cost	cost	ride	rode	ridden
cut	cut	cut	ring	rang	rung
do	did	done	rise	rose	risen
draw	drew	drawn	run	ran	run
dream	dreamed / dreamt	dreamed / dreamt	say	said	said
drink	drank	drunk	see	saw	seen
drive	drove	driven	sell	sold	sold
eat	ate	eaten	send	sent	sent
fall	fell	fallen	shake	shook	shaken
feed	fed	fed	sing	sang	sung
feel	felt	felt	sit	sat	sat
fight	fought	fought	sleep	slept	slept
find	found	found	speak	spoke	spoken
fit	fit	fit	spend	spent	spent
fly	flew	flown	stand	stood	stood
forget	forgot	forgotten	steal	stole	stolen
get	got	gotten	swim	swam	swum
give	gave	given	take	took	taken
go	went	gone	teach	taught	taught
grow	grew	grown	tell	told	told
have	had	had	think	thought	thought
hear	heard	heard	throw	threw	thrown
hit	hit	hit	understand	understood	understood
hold	held	held	wake up	woke up	woken up
hurt	hurt	hurt	wear	wore	worn
keep	kept	kept	win	won	won
know	knew	known	write	wrote	written

Verb tense review: present, past, and future

 THE PRESENT OF BE

Statements

I	am	
You We They	are	late.
He She It	is	

 THE SIMPLE PRESENT TENSE

Statements

I You We They	speak English.
He She	speaks English.

Yes / no questions

Do	I you we they	know them?
Does	he she	eat meat?

Short answers

Yes,	I you we they	do.
	he she it	does.

No,	I you we they	don't.
	he she it	doesn't.

Information questions

What do	you we they	need?
When does	he she it	start?
Who	wants needs likes	this book?

 THE PRESENT CONTINUOUS

Statements

I	am	watching TV.
You We They	are	studying English.
He She It	is	arriving now.

Yes / no questions

Am	I	
Are	you we they	going too fast?
Is	he she it	

Short answers

Yes,	I	am.
	you	are.
	he she it	is.
	we they	are.

No,	I'm not.
	you aren't / you're not.
	he isn't / he's not.
	she isn't / she's not.
	it isn't / it's not.
	we aren't / we're not.
	they aren't / they're not.

Information questions

What	are	you we they	doing?
When	is	he she it	leaving?
Where	am	I	staying tonight?
Who	is		driving?

 THE PAST OF BE

Statements

I He She It	was late.
We You They	were early.

Yes / no questions

Was	I he she it	on time?
Were	we you they	in the same class?

Short answers

Yes,	I he she it	was.
	we you they	were.

No,	I he she it	wasn't.
	we you they	weren't.

Information questions

Where	were	we? you? they?	
When	was	he she it	here?
Who	were	they?	
Who	was	he? she? it?	

5 THE SIMPLE PAST TENSE

Many verbs are irregular in the simple past tense.
See the list of irregular verbs on page A5.

Statements

I You He She It We They	stopped working.

I You He She It We They	didn't start again.

Yes / no questions

Did	I you he she it we they	make a good dinner?

Short answers

Yes,	I you he she it we they	did.

No,	I you he she it we they	didn't.

Information questions

When did	I you he she it we they	read that?
Who		called?

6 THE FUTURE WITH BE GOING TO

Statements

I'm You're He's She's It's We're They're	going to	be here soon.

I'm You're He's She's It's We're They're	not going to	be here soon.

Yes / no questions

Are	you we they	going to want coffee?
Am	I	going to be late?
Is	he she it	going to arrive on time?

Short answers

Yes,	I	am.
	you	are.
	he she it	is.
	we they	are.

No,	I'm not.
	you aren't / you're not.
	he isn't / he's not.
	she isn't / she's not.
	it isn't / it's not.
	we aren't / we're not.
	they aren't / they're not.

Information questions

What	are	you we they	going to see?
When	is	he she it	going to shop?
Where	am	I	going to stay tomorrow?
Who	is		going to call?

GRAMMAR
BOOSTER

2A

GRAMMAR BOOSTER

The *Grammar Booster* is optional. It provides more explanation and practice, as well as additional grammar concepts.

UNIT 1   Lesson 1

A **Complete the sentences with the present perfect or the simple past tense.**

I _____ in São Paulo, Brazil all my life. However, I _____ to a lot of other
   1. live   2. be

places too. I _____ to Europe three times. In 1999, I _____ to Amsterdam,
    3. fly   4. go

Vienna, and Prague. It _____ a wonderful trip. I _____ Europe again in 2000
       5. be   6. visit

and 2003. On that trip, I _____ the Eiffel Tower in Paris, _____ sightseeing
        7. climb   8. go

in London, and _____ a bullfight in Madrid. Of course, I _____ all over
      9. see   10. travel

Latin America too. In 2004, I _____ the United States and Canada for the first time. I
          11. tour

_____ to Asia, but I'd really like to go.
  12. be / not

The present perfect: information questions with <u>What</u> or <u>Which</u> and a noun

Use <u>What</u> or <u>Which</u> and the present perfect to ask for information about an indefinite time in the past.

 What (OR Which) languages **have you studied**?
 What (OR Which) countries **have you visited**?
 What (OR Which) dishes **have you tried**?

B **Use the topics to write questions with <u>What</u> or <u>Which</u> in the present perfect. Then write answers to the questions in your own way.**

 1. (big cities) _What big cities have you visited_ _____?

  Answer: _____.

 2. (new songs) _____?

  Answer: _____.

 3. (restaurants) _____?

  Answer: _____.

 4. (airlines) _____?

  Answer: _____.

 5. (movies) _____?

  Answer: _____.

UNIT 1 Lesson 2

The present perfect: use and placement of yet and already

Use <u>yet</u> in present perfect questions and negative statements. Put <u>yet</u> at the end of the sentence.

questions
Have you read the book **yet**?

negative statements
I haven't read the book **yet**.

Use <u>already</u> in present perfect questions and affirmative statements. Put <u>already</u> before the main verb or at the end of the sentence.

questions
Have you **already** read the book?
OR Have you read the book **already**?

affirmative statements
I've **already** read the book.
OR I've read the book **already**.

BE CAREFUL!

Don't use <u>yet</u> in present perfect affirmative statements.
DON'T SAY Yes, I've read the book ~~yet~~.

Don't use <u>already</u> in present perfect negative statements.
DON'T SAY No, I haven't ~~already~~ read the book.

A Rewrite each statement or question with <u>already</u> or <u>yet</u>.

1. (yet) Has she finished the book? _____?

2. (yet) They haven't seen the movie. _____.

3. (already) We've tried wild rice several times. _____.

4. (already) Has your father left _____?

B Rewrite each sentence with <u>already</u> or <u>yet</u>.

1. I haven't had dinner. _____.

2. She's been to London, Berlin, and Rome. _____.

3. They haven't called home. _____.

4. We've finished our class. _____.

The present perfect: <u>ever</u>, <u>never</u>, and <u>before</u>

Use <u>ever</u> in questions. Do not use <u>ever</u> in affirmative statements.

Have you **ever** made sushi?

Yes, I have. OR Yes, I've made it.
(NOT Yes, I've ~~ever~~ made it.)

Use <u>never</u> in negative short answers and statements.

Have you ever made sushi?

No, I **never** have.
OR No, I've **never** made sushi.

You can use <u>before</u> with or without <u>ever</u> and <u>never</u> in present perfect sentences and questions.

I've been to South Africa **before**.
I've **never** tried ceviche **before**.
Have you **ever** made chocolate cake **before**?

In very informal speech, <u>ever</u> is sometimes used to strongly emphasize <u>never</u>. The meaning of <u>ever</u> is similar to "in my whole life."

I've **never ever** made sushi!

C ▷ **Answer the questions, using real information. If the answer is <u>yes</u>, write when this happened.**

1. Have you ever gone on a cruise? _____.

2. Have you ever tried Indian food? _____.

3. Have you ever been to Hawaii? _____.

4. Have you ever met a famous person? _____.

5. Have you ever gone scuba diving? _____.

▶ **UNIT 2   Lesson 1**

┌─ **The present perfect and the present perfect continuous: unfinished actions** ──────

Unfinished actions are those that began in the past, continue in the present, and may continue into the future. Here are three ways to talk about unfinished (or continuous) actions:

1. the present perfect with <u>since</u>: Use <u>since</u> with a stated start time in the past.
   I've lived here **since** 2001. (2001 is the stated start time. I still live here.)

2. the present perfect with <u>for</u>: Use <u>for</u> to describe the period of time from its start until the present.
   I've lived here **for** five years. (Emphasis is on the five-year period. I still live here.)

3. the present perfect continuous with <u>for</u> and <u>since</u>: Form the present perfect continuous with the present perfect of <u>be</u> and a present participle.
   I've been living here since 2001. OR **I've been living** here for five years.

A ▷ **Complete each statement with the present perfect continuous.**

1. *Seabiscuit* _____ at the Park Lane Classic Cinema since April.
   play

2. Robert _____ in the ticket holders' line for a pretty long time.
   wait

3. People _____ violence in movies since the sixties.
   worry about

4. I _____ that movie with everyone for weeks.
   talk about

5. We _____ to this movie theater for two years.
   come

B ▷ **Read the sentences. Check if the sentence describes an unfinished (continuous) action. Then rewrite those sentences in the present perfect continuous.**

☐ 1. The Grants have lived in Buenos Aires since the late seventies.

☐ 2. Their friends have already visited them.

☐ 3. We have waited to see you for three years.

☐ 4. This is the first time I've visited Paris.

☐ 5. We have eaten in that great Indian restaurant for years.

☐ 6. Has she ever met your teacher?

☐ 7. How long have you studied Chinese?

☐ 8. My children have just come back from the movies.

Add –ing to the base form of the verb.

speak → speaking

If the base form ends in a silent –e, drop the –e and add –ing.

have → having

In verbs of one syllable, if the last three letters are a consonant-vowel-consonant (C-V-C) series, double the last consonant and then add –ing.

C V C
s i t → sitting

BE CAREFUL! Don't double the last consonant in words that end in –w, –x, or –y.

flow → flowing
fix → fixing
pay → paying

In verbs of more than one syllable that end in a consonant-vowel-consonant series, double the last consonant only if the stress is on the last syllable.

contról → controlling   BUT órder → ordering

Write the present participle for the following base forms.

1. find _____

2. be _____

3. lose _____

4. put _____

5. get _____

6. say _____

7. write _____

8. go _____

9. make _____

10. fix _____

11. know _____

12. speak _____

13. hear _____

14. let _____

15. come _____

16. leave _____

17. drive _____

18. meet _____

19. blow _____

20. give _____

21. run _____

22. forget _____

23. eat _____

24. pay _____

25. stand _____

26. think _____

27. buy _____

28. see _____

29. begin _____

30. tell _____

31. bring _____

32. take _____

┌─ Will **and** be going to ─────────────────────────────────

Use **will** or **be going to** for predictions about the future. The meaning is the same.

> It'll **rain** tomorrow.
> It's **going to rain** tomorrow.

Use **be going to** when you already have a plan for the future.

> A: Are you **going to come** to class tomorrow?
> B: No, I'm **going to go** to the beach instead.

Use **will** to talk about the immediate future when you do not already have a plan.

> Maybe I'll **go** to the beach this weekend.

Use **will** for willingness.

> I'll **eat** meat, but I **won't eat** vegetables.

A **Write five sentences about your plans for this weekend.**

_____.

_____.

_____.

_____.

_____.

B **Write five sentences using** will **for willingness on one of the following topics: types of exercise you are willing to do; types of food you are willing to eat for breakfast; types of clothes you are NOT willing to wear.**

_____.

_____.

_____.

_____.

_____.

Degrees of obligation

have to / must

Use <u>have to</u> (OR <u>have got to</u>) or <u>must</u>* to express obligation. These modals suggest there is no other choice of action available.

> Students **must** take this exam to graduate.
> If you want to arrive before 8:00, you **have to** (OR **have got to**) take the 6:00 train.

had better

Use <u>had better</u> to mean there is a consequence for not doing something.

> You'd **better** make a reservation. The hotel is very popular.

be supposed to

Use <u>be supposed to</u> to mean that other people expect you to take this action.

> We're **supposed to** check out by twelve, but I think we can get a late checkout if we ask.

should / ought to†

Use <u>should</u> or <u>ought to</u> to state an opinion or give advice.

> You **should** (OR **ought to**) stay at the Milton Hotel. It's close to town and very good.

could

Use <u>could</u> to suggest an alternative action.

> They **could** stay at the Festival Hotel if there are no rooms at the Milton.

BE CAREFUL!

In the negative, <u>must not</u> (OR <u>mustn't</u>) expresses a prohibition.

> You **must not** smoke here. = Don't smoke here.

However, <u>don't have to</u> expresses a lack of obligation.

> You **don't have to** show your passport to cash a check.

* <u>Must</u> is very formal and is likely to be used by a person in authority (a teacher to students, for example). <u>Have got to</u> is often used in spoken English with the same meaning as <u>have to</u>.

† <u>Ought to</u> has the same meaning as <u>should</u>, but is slightly less formal. Don't use <u>ought to</u> in questions or negative statements.

 Choose the sentence closer in meaning to each numbered statement or question.

1. Do you think the Milton Hotel is a good place to stay?

   a. Do you think I should stay at the Milton?
   b. Do you think I have to stay at the Milton?

2. If you don't have your luggage ticket, the bellman won't give you your luggage.

   a. You could give the bellman the ticket.
   b. You must give the bellman the ticket.

3. They don't accept credit cards in this hotel. They only accept cash.

   a. You have to pay with cash.
   b. You'd better pay with cash.

4. When I made the reservation, I asked for a suite.

    a. They mustn't give me a suite.

    b. They're supposed to give me a suite.

5. Don't wear shorts in the restaurant.

    a. You must not wear shorts in the restaurant.

    b. You don't have to wear shorts in the restaurant.

UNIT 4 *Lesson 1*

The past continuous: uses

The past continuous describes an action that was continuous until (and possibly after) the moment at which another action took place. The words <u>when</u> or <u>while</u> are often used with the past continuous.

> He **was talking** on the phone when the storm began.
> While I **was living** in Chile, I got married.

The past continuous also describes two continuing actions occurring in the same period of time.

> While she **was driving**, her husband **was reading** the newspaper.
> They **were eating**, and the music **was playing**.

The past continuous is also used when we report someone else's words.

> They said, "We are arriving at three o'clock."　→　They said they **were arriving** at three o'clock.

A **Write questions with the past continuous.**

1. (**YOU**) _____ ?

"She was taking a test at school."

2. (**YOU**) _____ ?

"I was talking to my mother on the phone."

3. (**YOU**) _____ ?

"Mr. Kemp was driving."

4. (**YOU**) _____ ?

"At three o'clock? The teacher was teaching an art class."

5. (**YOU**) _____ ?

"I'm not sure. I think they were cooking."

UNIT 4 Lesson 2

Direct objects

Verbs are either transitive or intransitive. Transitive verbs have direct objects. In English sentences, direct object nouns and pronouns come after the verb.

    I love **my car**.   She bought **new tires**.   They painted **it**.

Many phrasal verbs are called "separable" because the direct object can come before or after the particle.

    They **dropped off** their car. They **dropped** their car **off**.

BUT: When the direct object is a pronoun, it must come before the particle.

    They **dropped** it **off**.   NOT They ~~dropped off~~ it.

subject pronouns	object pronouns
I	me
you	you
he	him
she	her
it	it
we	us
they	them

A Complete the conversations with phrasal verbs and object pronouns.

1. **A:** Can I drop the car off early?

   B: Yes, you can _____ before nine o'clock.

2. **A:** Don't forget to fill the car up with gas and get oil.

   B: Don't worry. I'll _____ after English class.

3. **A:** I don't know which switch turns on the headlights.

   B: _____ with this switch.

4. **A:** How do I turn the air-conditioning off? It's freezing in here.

   B: The air-conditioning? You can _____ with that switch over there.

5. **A:** I need to pick the car up soon. What time will it be ready?

   B: Let's see. It'll be ready at 4:00. Please _____ then.

UNIT 5 Lesson 1

Non-count nouns: containers, quantifiers, and other modifiers

REMEMBER: Count nouns name things you can count individually. They have singular and plural forms. Non-count nouns name things you cannot count individually. They don't have plural forms.

Containers, quantifiers, and other modifiers make non-count nouns countable.

    two kilos of rice   **three cups of** coffee

The following is a list of common containers and quantifiers:

a kilo	a gallon	a carton	a bottle	a cup
a gram	a liter	a package	a jar	a spoonful
a pound	a bag	a container	a tube	a slice
an ounce	a box	a can	a bar	a loaf

A Make each of these non-count nouns countable. Use quantifiers or container words.

1. rice _____

2. chocolate _____

3. milk _____

4. toothpaste _____

5. shampoo _____

6. shaving cream _____

7. body lotion _____

Too many, too much, and enough

The word <u>too</u> indicates a quantity that is excessive—more than someone wants or needs. Use <u>enough</u> to say if something is satisfactory.

Use <u>too many</u> (and <u>not too many</u>) for count nouns.

There are **too many customers** waiting in line.

Use <u>too much</u> (and <u>not too much</u>) for non-count nouns.

There's **too much toothpaste** on the toothbrush.

Use <u>enough</u> (and <u>not enough</u>) for both count and non-count nouns.

There's **enough shampoo**, but there aren't **enough razors**.

B Complete each sentence with <u>too many</u>, <u>too much</u>, or <u>enough</u>.

1. Let's make a nice dessert. Do we have _____ milk in the fridge?

2. This coffee has _____ sugar. It's awful.

3. It's not a good idea to buy _____ fruit. We're not going to be home for a few days.

4. This menu has _____ choices. I can't make up my mind.

5. Check the bathroom shelf to see if we have _____ soap. Mom and Dad are coming to visit.

6. I don't like when there are _____ brands. I can't decide which one to buy.

7. There's no way to get a haircut today. _____ people had the same idea!

8. I don't have _____ gas in the car for a long trip. Could you please get some when you go out?

9. They don't want to spend _____ money on their vacation. They're going camping.

┌─ Indefinite pronouns: <u>something</u>, <u>anything</u>, and <u>nothing</u> ─────────────┐

Use <u>something</u> in affirmative statements.

There's **something** in this box.

Use <u>anything</u> in negative statements.

There **isn't anything** in the fridge.

Use <u>something</u> or <u>anything</u> in <u>yes</u> / <u>no</u> questions.

Is there **something** we should talk about? Is **anything** wrong?

<u>Nothing</u> is the equivalent of <u>not anything</u>. Don't use <u>nothing</u> in negative statements.

There isn**'t anything** in the fridge. = There's **nothing** in the fridge.
NOT There ~~isn't nothing~~ in the fridge.

└──┘

A **Choose the correct indefinite pronoun to complete each sentence.**

1. I need to go to the store to buy _____.
   something / anything

2. There is _____ I can do to help.
   something / anything

3. There isn't _____ you can do to make yourself taller.
   something / anything

4. A skin doctor can tell you _____ about how to use sunscreen.
   something / anything

5. They have _____ that helps you lose weight.
   something / anything

6. My dentist recommended _____ to whiten my teeth.
   something / anything

7. There's _____ that can make you look young again.
   anything / nothing

8. They can't get _____ to eat there after ten o'clock.
   anything / nothing

🎧 TOP NOTCH POP LYRICS FOR 2A AND 2B

Greetings and Small Talk [Unit 1]

You look so familiar. Have we met before?
I don't think you're from around here.
It might have been two weeks ago, but I'm not sure.
Has it been a month or a year?
I have a funny feeling that I've met you twice.
That's what they call déjà vu.
You were saying something friendly, trying to be nice,
and now you're being friendly too.
One look, one word.
It's the friendliest sound that I've ever heard.
Thanks for your greeting.
I'm glad this meeting occurred.

(CHORUS)
Greetings and small talk
make the world go round.
On every winding road I've walked,
this is what I've found.

Have you written any letters to your friends back home?
Have you had a chance to do that?
Have you spoken to your family on the telephone?
Have you taken time for a chat?
Bow down, shake hands.
Do whatever you do in your native land.
I'll be happy to greet you
in any way that you understand.

(CHORUS)
Have you seen the latest movie out of Hollywood?
Have you read about it yet?
If you haven't eaten dinner, are you in the mood
for a meal you won't forget?
Bow down, shake hands.
Do whatever you do in your native land.
I'll be happy to greet you
in any way that you understand.

(CHORUS)

Better Late Than Never [Unit 2]

Where have you been? I've waited for you.
I'd rather not say how long.
The movie began one hour ago.
How did you get the time all wrong?
Well, I got stuck in traffic, and when I arrived,
I couldn't find a parking place.
Did you buy the tickets? You're kidding—for real?
Let me pay you back, in that case.

(CHORUS)
Sorry I'm late.
I know you've waited here forever.
How long has it been?
It's always better late than never.

When that kind of movie comes to the big screen,
it always attracts a crowd.
And I've always wanted to see it with you,
but it looks like we've missed it now.
I know what you're saying, but actually,
I would rather watch a video.
So why don't we rent it and bring it back home?
Let's get in the car and go.

(CHORUS)
Didn't you mention, when we made our plans,
that you've seen this movie recently?
It sounds so dramatic, and I'm so upset,
I'd rather see a comedy!
Well, which comedy do you recommend?
It really doesn't matter to me.
I still haven't seen *The World and a Day*.
I've heard that one is pretty funny.

(CHORUS)

Wheels around the World [Unit 4]

Was I going too fast
or a little too slow?
I was looking out the window,
and I just don't know.
I must have turned the steering wheel
a little too far
when I drove into the bumper
of that luxury car.
Oh no!
How awful!
What a terrible day!
I'm sorry to hear that.
Are you OK?

(CHORUS)
Wheels around the World
are waiting here with your car.
Pick it up.
Turn it on.
Play the radio.
Wheels around the World—
"helping you to go far."
You can drive anywhere.
Buckle up and go.

Did I hit the red sedan,
or did it hit me?
I was talking on the cell phone
in my SUV.
Nothing was broken,
and no one was hurt,
but I did spill some coffee
on my favorite shirt.
Oh no!
Thank goodness
you're still alive!
I'm so happy that
you survived.

(CHORUS)
What were you doing when you hit that tree?
I was racing down the mountain, and the brakes failed me.
How did it happen? Was the road still wet?
Well, there might have been a danger sign,
but I forget.
The hood popped open and the door fell off.
The headlights blinked and the engine coughed.
The side-view mirror had a terrible crack.
The gearshift broke. Can I bring the car back?
Oh no!
Thank goodness
you're still alive!
I'm so happy that
you survived.

(CHORUS)

The Colors of Love [Unit 7]

Are you sick and tired of working hard day and night?
Do you like to look at the world in shades of black and white?
Your life can still be everything that you were dreaming of.
Just take a look around you and see all the colors of love.
You wake up every morning and go through the same old grind.
You don't know how the light at the window could be so unkind.
If blue is the color that you choose when the road is rough,
you know you really need to believe in the colors of love.

(CHORUS)
The colors of love
are as beautiful as a rainbow.
The colors of love
shine on everyone in the world.

Are negative thoughts and emotions painful to express?
They're just tiny drops in the ocean of happiness.
And these are the feelings you must learn to rise above.
Your whole life is a picture you paint with the colors of love.

(CHORUS)

To Each His Own [Unit 8]

He doesn't care for Dali.
The colors are too bright.
He says that Picasso
got everything just right.
She can't stand the movies
that are filmed in Hollywood.
She likes Almodóvar.
She thinks he's really good.
He's inspired by everything
she thinks is second-rate.
She's moved and fascinated
by the things he loves to hate.
He's crazy about art that only
turns her heart to stone.
I guess that's why they say
to each his own.
He likes pencil drawings.
She prefers photographs.
He takes her to the art museum,
but she just laughs and laughs.
He loves the Da Vinci
that's hanging by the door.
She prefers the modern art
that's lying on the floor.
"No kidding! You'll love it. Just wait and see.
It's perfect in every way."
She shakes her head. "It's not for me.
It's much too old and gray."
She thinks he has the worst taste
that the world has ever known.
I guess that's why they say
to each his own.
But when it's time to say good-bye,
they both feel so alone.
I guess that's why they say
to each his own.

Workbook

Joan Saslow ■ Allen Ascher

with Terra Brockman

PEARSON
Longman

UNIT **1**

Greetings and Small Talk

TOPIC PREVIEW

1 Look at the pictures. Write the correct greeting under each picture. Use words from the box.

| bow | hug | kiss | shake hands |

1. _____   2. _____   3. _____   4. _____

2 Complete the conversation. Write the letter on the line.

A: You look familiar. Have we met before?

B: ____
   1.

A: Aren't you from Mexico?

B: ____
   2.

A: You know, I think we met at Joan's house last weekend.

B: ____
   3.

A: Yes, that's right. What have you been up to?

B: ____
   4.

a. Now I remember. You work with Joan.

b. As a matter of fact, I am.

c. Not too much.

d. I don't think so. I'm not from around here.

3 Read the conversation in Exercise 2 again. Circle the subjects they talk about.

family   religion   job   age   weather   nationality

4 WHAT ABOUT YOU? When you meet someone new, what subjects do you talk about? Put a ✔ next to the topics you usually talk about. Put an ✗ next to the topics you don't like to talk about.

_____ 1. my family   _____ 4. my age   _____ 7. politics

_____ 2. my religion   _____ 5. my hometown or country   _____ 8. my job

_____ 3. the weather   _____ 6. sports   _____ 9. other: _____

LESSON 1

6 Complete each sentence with the present perfect. Use contractions when possible.

1. A: _____ any coffee
   you / have
   today?

   B: Yes, _____ two cups.
   I / have

2. A: _____ to any
   you / be
   foreign countries?

   B: Yes, _____ to Spain
   we / be
   and Morocco.

3. A: _____ this week?
   you / exercise

   B: Yes, _____ to the gym
   I / go
   twice.

4. A: _____ any good
   you / read
   books lately?

   B: No, _____ very busy.
   I / be

7 WHAT ABOUT YOU? Complete the questions with the correct form of the verbs from the box. Use each verb only once. Then write your own responses. When you answer yes, add specific information, using the simple past tense.

do	be	eat	meet	see

1. "Have you _____ any good movies lately?"

   (YOU) _____.

2. "Have you _____ any famous people?"

   (YOU) _____.

3. "Have you _____ to Europe?"

   (YOU) _____.

4. "Have you _____ lunch today?"

   (YOU) _____.

5. "Have you _____ your homework today?"

   (YOU) _____.

8 ▸ **Complete the conversation with the present perfect or the simple past tense. Use contractions when possible.**

Joe: _____ this tour before? I hear it's great.
       1. you / take

Trish: Yes, I have. I _____ to Russia with this group two years ago.
                        2. come

   It _____ a wonderful trip. _____ here before?
       3. be   **4. you / be**

Joe: Yes, I _____ Moscow in 2002, but I _____ much of the city.
             5. visit   **6. not / see**

   It _____ a business trip. I'm really excited about *this* trip!
       7. be

Trish: Me too. I _____ the brochures several times last night.
                  8. read

   I can't wait to see all these places again. By the way,

   _____ Peter, our tour guide?
         9. you / meet

Joe: No, but I'd like to.

Trish: Come. I'll introduce you.

LESSON 2

9 ▸ **Complete the sentences. Circle the correct words.**

1. Have you (ever / yet) visited the art museums in Paris?

2. I haven't been to the opera (already / yet).

3. Who is she? I haven't seen her (ever / before).

4. Has Evan (yet / ever) tried ceviche (before / already)?

5. We've only been here one day, but we've (already / yet) taken a lot of pictures.

6. I'm sorry. I haven't finished the job (already / yet).

7. He's only fourteen years old, but he's (already / yet) traveled all over the world.

10 ▸ **Complete each conversation. Write questions or answers in the present perfect. Use ever, before, already, or yet.**

1. A: Has Ted taken a tour of the Statue of Liberty yet?

   B: Yes. He _____.

2. A: _____?

   B: No. Actually this is my first time to London.

3. A: _____?

   B: No, but they plan to go to the top of the Sears Tower tomorrow.

4. A: Has Lisa ever tried Turkish food?

   B: Yes. She _____ several times.

11 Look at Anne Marie and Gilbert's To-Do List for their vacation in Toronto. Anne Marie has checked what they've already done.

✔ – take a tour of the University

✔ – meet Michel for dinner on Spadina Avenue

– visit the Bata Shoe Museum

✔ – see a musical downtown

– take a boat trip around Toronto Harbor

✔ – go shopping at the Eaton Centre

Now finish Anne Marie's postcard to her friend. Write what she and Gilbert have already done and what they haven't done yet. Use the present perfect.

Dear Agnes,   Sunday, August 6

Gilbert and I are having a wonderful time in Toronto.
We've done so many things! _____
_____
_____
_____
_____
_____
_____
_____
_____
_____

See you when we get back.

Love,
Anne Marie

LESSON 3

12 Read the information about greetings in Asia. Then read the statements and check <u>true</u>, <u>false</u>, or <u>no information</u>.

GETTING GREETINGS RIGHT

The traditional greeting in Asia is a bow. In fact, there are different types of bows used in greetings throughout Asia. For example, in Japan, China, and Korea, people bow, but in Japan the bow is usually lower. In India and nearby countries in South Asia, most people put their hands together and bow just a little.

While each Asian culture has its own traditional special greeting, these days, don't be surprised if people in Asia just shake your hand.

SOURCE: www.factmonster.com and *Kiss, Bow, or Shake Hands*.

	true	false	no information
1. People in China, Japan, and Korea bow when they greet someone.	☐	☐	☐
2. In Korea, people usually bow lower than in Japan.	☐	☐	☐
3. In India, you shouldn't touch the person you are greeting.	☐	☐	☐
4. People in many places in South Asia use a similar greeting.	☐	☐	☐

13 WHAT ABOUT YOU? **Complete these sentences about yourself.**

1. In this country, the most common greeting is _____.

2. When I greet someone for the first time, I usually _____.

3. When I greet a family member or close friend, I usually _____.

FACTOID

History of the Handshake
Shaking hands was a way of making sure that people were not carrying a weapon such as a knife or sword. When you shook hands, you were saying, "Look, I don't have a weapon. I trust you. Let's be friends."

SOURCE: www.canadaone.com

LESSON 4

14 George Ruez is a true adventurer. He has done a lot of things in his life. Write questions about George. Use the present perfect with <u>ever</u> or <u>before</u>.

1. _Has George ever been to Paris_____? (Paris)

2. _____? (horseback riding)

3. _____? (Mt. Everest)

4. _____? (guinea pig)

5. _____? (octopus)

6. _____? (Mt. Kilimanjaro)

7. _____? (sailing)

8. _____? (Buenos Aires)

15 Look at the pictures showing some of the things George has done. Now answer the questions from Exercise 14. Use the present perfect with <u>yet</u> or <u>already</u>.

1. _____.

2. _____.

3. _____.

4. _____.

5. _____.

6. _____.

7. _____.

8. _____.

GRAMMAR
BOOSTER

A ▸ **Read the first sentence. Then decide if the second sentence is true (T) or false (F).**

1. I've never been to Lebanon.   _____ I went to Lebanon a long time ago.

2. He hasn't been to Barbados yet.   _____ He was in Barbados last week.

3. She's already left for Tokyo.   _____ She is going to Tokyo.

4. She has never been to Mexico before.   _____ This is her first visit to Mexico.

5. We have visited Bangkok several times.   _____ We've been to Bangkok before.

B ▸ **Look at the answers. Write questions with What (OR Which).**

1. **A:** _____ ?

   B: I've tried Hungarian food and German food.

2. **A:** _____ ?

   B: We've been to Morocco and Egypt.

3. **A:** _____ ?

   B: He's gone to the Metropolitan Museum of Art and the Museum of Modern Art.

4. **A:** _____ ?

   B: She's studied Spanish and English.

5. **A:** _____ ?

   B: I've visited Budapest and Prague.

6. **A:** _____ ?

   B: We've seen two operas—*Carmen* and *Othello*.

C ▸ **Complete the conversation with the present perfect or the simple past tense. Use contractions when possible.**

A: Welcome to Rome! When _____ you _____ ?

                                                      1. arrive

B: A few days ago.

A: Oh, that's great. _____ you _____ sightseeing yet?

                                                         2. go

B: Yes, a little. I _____ Piazza Navona already and I _____ a tour of

                          3. see   **4. take**

   the Coliseum yesterday.

A: Great! _____ you _____ to Vatican City yet?

                                                       5. be

B: Yes, as a matter of fact. I _____ there on Thursday.

                                        6. go

A: How about Italian food? _____ you _____ any real Italian

                                                             7. eat

   pizza or pasta yet?

B: I _____ pasta with seafood last night. But I _____ any calamari yet.

              8. have   **9. not try**

   I _____ so many times that's something I shouldn't miss.

             10. hear

A: Oh, yes! The calamari here is excellent. And Rome is a great city. Enjoy your stay!

B: Thanks.

D Rewrite the sentences, using the word(s) in parentheses.

1. Have you been to Taiwan? (before)

   _____?

2. Josefina hasn't had her lunch. (yet)

   _____.

3. He was born in Egypt, but he hasn't seen the pyramids. (never)

   _____.

4. Has Gus taken a tour of the city? (before)

   _____?

5. I haven't tried octopus. (never)

   _____.

6. Have you had anything to eat? (yet)

   _____?

7. Have you been to the outdoor market? (ever, before)

   _____?

8. Prague is so beautiful! I haven't been here. (never, before)

   _____.

9. She's finished college. (already)

   _____.

E WHAT ABOUT YOU? Answer the questions with sentences about yourself. Give details about your experiences.

1. "What's an unusual food you've tried?"

   YOU _____.

2. "What's an interesting country or city you've been to?"

   YOU _____.

3. "What's an exciting sport you've played?"

   YOU _____.

4. "What's a wonderful book you've read?"

   YOU _____.

JUST FOR FUN

FIGURE IT OUT! Rearrange the letters of the following phrase to form the name of a famous building in England. (Hint: 3 words)

ONE OLD FORT NOW

2 The drawings show gestures and customs that should or should not be used in certain countries. Unscramble the letters to form the name of each country.

1. In _____, you should never touch a person, even a child, on the head. (ADLITAHN)

Thank you very much!

2. In _____, open a gift immediately and thank the person who gave it to you. (RCEDAUO)

3. In _____, you should cover your mouth when you're using a toothpick. (AWINAT)

Say, how much money do you make?

4. In the _____, it's better not to ask people personal questions such as how much money they make. (DTEIUN NGMIKOD) (2 words)

5. In _____, you should take off your shoes before entering someone's home. (AANPJ)

6. In _____, putting a coat on a chair in a restaurant is considered rude. (SUASIR)

Answer to Exercise 1: TOWER OF LONDON

UNIT 2

Movies and Entertainment

TOPIC PREVIEW

 Choose the correct response. Circle the letter.

1. "Did you see *Aliens Alive* when it came out last summer?"

   a. I'd rather watch the tube. b. No. I missed it.

2. "I really want to see the new Jackie Chan movie. What do you say?"

   a. Have you already seen it? b. I'm not in the mood for an action film.

3. "How about we go see a classic movie?"

   a. Deal! b. They said it was great.

4. "Would you like some Chinese food after the movie?"

   a. Actually, I'd rather have Italian food. b. How about it?

 Write the genre of the movie under the picture.

1. _____ 2. _____ 3. _____ 4. _____ 5. _____

 Read the newspaper movie listings. Choose a genre that best describes each movie. Write the title of another movie of that genre you've seen.

ESSEX TIMES

Friday, May 22   ENTERTAINMENT   page 39

The Fearless Fighter

You'll be on the edge of your seat. Don't miss this exciting adventure! But don't bring the kids—a little too violent.
—Josephine Potter, NewsNow

Edgewood Theater:
6:00, 8:15, 10:30

Myra's Day

Spend the day with Myra. You'll laugh so hard you might fall out of your seat!
—Roger Sullivan, Movietime

Plaza Cinemas:
2:00, 4:00, 6:00, 8:00, 10:00

Goodnight, Mariana

Mariana tries to find her long lost mother. Her search takes her all over the country. Very sad and touching. Based on a true story.
—Oscar Wilson, www.OWfilms.com

Castle Theater:
1:45, 4:00, 6:15, 8:30

Genre: _____ Genre: _____ Genre: _____

Movie: _____ Movie: _____ Movie: _____

WHAT ABOUT YOU? **Which of the movies from the listing in Exercise 3 would you most like to see? Why?**

LESSON 1

 Look at the pictures. Then complete the conversation.

Patty: Hi, Rosemary. Sorry I'm late. Have you been here long?

Rosemary: For about twenty minutes. What happened?

Patty: Well, first _____. I ran to catch it, but it pulled away.
                                        1.

And _____, because it was raining. So, I went back home to
              2.

get my car. Then _____. Finally I got here, but _____.
                          3.   **4.**

It took me about ten minutes before I found one!

Rosemary: Well, you're here now. Let's go see the movie!

6 **Complete the posting from an online movie chat room. Use <u>since</u> or <u>for</u>.**

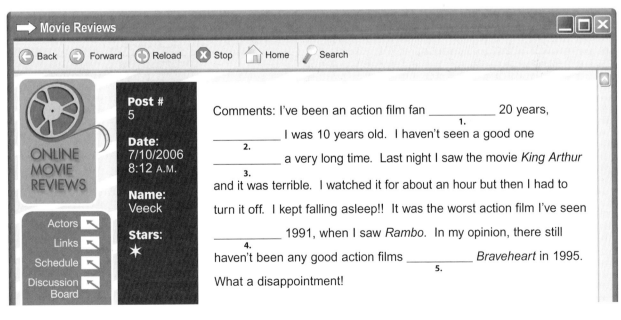

Movie Reviews

Back | Forward | Reload | Stop | Home | Search

ONLINE MOVIE REVIEWS

Post # 5

Date: 7/10/2006 8:12 A.M.

Name: Veeck

Stars: ★

Actors | Links | Schedule | Discussion Board

Comments: I've been an action film fan _____ 20 years,
                                                              1.
_____ I was 10 years old. I haven't seen a good one
       2.
_____ a very long time. Last night I saw the movie *King Arthur*
       3.
and it was terrible. I watched it for about an hour but then I had to
turn it off. I kept falling asleep!! It was the worst action film I've seen
_____ 1991, when I saw *Rambo*. In my opinion, there still
       4.
haven't been any good action films _____ *Braveheart* in 1995.
                                                    5.
What a disappointment!

LESSON 2

7 Complete each statement about movie genres. Write the letter on the line.

1. Fighting and killing are common in __e__ .
2. In the past, ____ were drawn by hand, but a lot of them are now done on the computer.
3. A ____ tells a story with singing and dancing.
4. A ____ gives facts and information about real people and events.
5. A ____ usually takes place in the future.
6. *Airplane* is a great ____. I can't stop laughing every time I watch it.
7. This courtroom ____ is a serious movie about life and death.
8. Scary things happen in ____ .

a. drama
b. documentary
c. science-fiction film
d. horror films
e. action films
f. animated films
g. musical
h. comedy

8 Look at Tom's favorite things and <u>least</u> favorite things.

Tom's Favorite Things

1. comedy
2. a trip to the beach
3. pop music
4. rice
5. going to the gym

Tom's <u>Least</u> Favorite Things

1. documentary
2. a trip to the mountains
3. classical music
4. pasta
5. going shopping

Now read each statement and circle <u>T</u> (true) or <u>F</u> (false), based on Tom's lists. Then write five true statements about yourself. Use <u>would rather</u>.

1. Tom would rather see a comedy than a documentary.   T   F

   (YOU) _____.

2. He'd rather take a trip to the mountains than to the beach.   T   F

   (YOU) _____.

3. He'd rather listen to classical music than pop music.   T   F

   (YOU) _____.

4. Tom would rather have rice than pasta.   T   F

   (YOU) _____.

5. He'd rather go to the gym than go shopping.   T   F

   (YOU) _____.

LESSON 3

 9 Read the online movie reviews and fill in the chart. Write the genre and choose at least two adjectives from the box that best describe the movie. Then write the name of a movie of the same genre that you've seen.

funny	boring	silly	violent	unforgettable	weird	interesting

THE REVIEW PAGES

THE ALIEN!

I was really looking forward to this: Martians take over a city in the year 2020. I usually love these kinds of movies, but *The Alien!* is just too strange for words. The story doesn't make sense. It was downright stupid!

—Kris Baker

SEARCH FOR THE LOST KINGDOM

This is going to be a blockbuster hit! The acting was terrific! A little too much killing for me, but it was still a great movie. I won't forget this movie for a long time!

—Ajay007

DAD'S BACK!

In *Dad's Back!*, Morgan Silva documents himself and his family for a whole month. It sounds boring, but you'll be surprised at how really humorous and entertaining the movie is. I strongly recommend this film to everyone out there.

—Marty1995

DON'T SCREAM NOW

A film about a killer monster is scary and exciting, right? Not this one! It was not interesting at all! Almost everyone gets killed, and still I couldn't stay awake! I'd rather have stayed home and read a book.

—Yasir

ONLINE

Movie title	Genre	Adjectives	Similar movie I've seen
The Alien!			
Search for the Lost Kingdom			
Dad's Back!			
Don't Scream Now			

10 **Complete the conversation. Write the letter on the line.**

A: Hi, Janelle. Seen any good movies recently?

B: _____
     1.

A: *Play Time*? What kind of movie is that?

B: _____
     2.

A: Really? What is it about?

B: _____
     3.

A: That doesn't sound very funny. Was it any good?

B: _____
     4.

A: The funniest? Wow! Who was in it?

B: _____
     5.

A: So you would recommend it?

B: _____
     6.

a. It was terrific. It might be the funniest film I've seen this year.

b. It's a comedy. You have to see it.

c. Oh, yes. I think you'd like it.

d. Yeah, I just saw *Play Time* at the Art Cinema.

e. It's about some high school kids who don't want to graduate.

f. It stars Wilson Grant—he was really hilarious.

 11 CHALLENGE. WHAT ABOUT YOU? **Write your <u>own</u> review about a movie you've seen. Use the reviews in Exercise 9 for support. In your review, try to answer the following questions: What kind of movie was it? What was it about? Who was in it? Was it good? Would you recommend it?**

LESSON 4

 12 Read the article. Then complete the statements, according to the information in the article. Circle the letter.

Children and Media Violence

Did you know that according to a recent study, children spend 6½ hours with the media* every day? Between the ages of 4 and 18, the average child sees 200,000 acts of violence on TV and other media, including 40,000 murders. Another study found that 61% of television programs show some violence, and 43% of these violent scenes are used to make people laugh. Also, 44% of the time, violent people in movies seem attractive or beautiful. In other media, like video games, 60 to 90% of the most popular games have violent subject matter. Other studies show that when children and young adults watch violent movies and play violent video games, they act more violently. As a result, these children see violence as a way to work out problems.

*Media in these studies include TV, movies, cartoons, video games, and the Internet.

SOURCE: http://www.mediafamily.org

1. Between the ages of 4 and 18, the average child sees ____.

   a. 40,000 television programs   **b.** 200,000 murders   **c.** 40,000 murders on TV

2. ____ of all TV shows contain violent scenes.

   a. More than half   **b.** Half   **c.** Less than half

3. Violence on TV is often meant to be seen as ____.

   a. unforgettable   **b.** funny   **c.** scary

4. People who are violent in movies are shown as ____.

   a. good-looking   **b.** silly   **c.** dangerous

5. Viewing violent movies and playing violent video games can make people ____.

   a. more violent   **b.** more boring   **c.** more beautiful

13 WHAT ABOUT YOU? Complete the Violence in the Media Survey.

☐ Violence in the Media Survey

1. Do you think there is too much violence in the media?   ☐ YES   ☐ NO
2. What types of media do you think show the most violence?

   [   ]

3. What kinds of TV shows and movies do you spend the most time watching? Rank these from 1 (most watched) to 8 (least watched).

   ☐ dramas
   ☐ comedies
   ☐ cartoons
   ☐ action
   ☐ music videos
   ☐ horror
   ☐ documentaries
   ☐ other   Please specify: [   ]

4. How many TV shows and movies that you see each week contain violent acts?

   ☐ 0–5
   ☐ 5–10
   ☐ 10–15
   ☐ 15–20
   ☐ over 20

5. I think that watching violent TV shows and movies . . .

   ☐ makes people more likely to act violently themselves.
   ☐ makes people less likely to behave violently themselves.
   ☐ has no effect on people's behavior.

Fill in the chart with the correct forms of the irregular verbs.

Base Form	Simple Past Tense	Past Participle	Present Participle
be	was / were	been	being
	ate		
go			
			having
		heard	
	met		
sit			
			speaking
take			
		written	
	paid		
			making

B **Read the first sentence. Then decide if the second sentence is true (T) or false (F).**

1. She's been living in Milan for two years. _____ She still lives in Milan.

2. She's lived in Milan for two years. _____ She no longer lives in Milan.

3. I've been renting a lot of DVDs lately. _____ I am still renting DVDs.

4. How long have you been watching that film? _____ You are still watching the film.

5. She's written a review of the new movie. _____ She's finished writing the review.

6. We've been waiting to see *Black Cat, White Cat.* _____ We have already seen *Black Cat, White Cat.*

C **WHAT ABOUT YOU? Answer the questions. Use your own words.**

1. "How long have you been studying English?"

   (YOU) _____ .

2. "How long have you lived in this city or town?"

   (YOU) _____ .

3. "Is there any movie you've been waiting to see?"

   (YOU) _____ .

Read about U.S. tennis star Serena Williams. Underline all the verbs in the present perfect. Circle all the time expressions with <u>since</u> or <u>for</u>.

tennis

Serena Williams

Serena Williams was born on September 26, 1981. She picked up her first tennis racket when she was four. Since then she has become one of the greatest tennis players in the world. Born in Michigan in the central part of the U.S., she moved to California when she was two. She has lived in Los Angeles for most of her life. She played her first tournament at age eight. Since then she has won many international competitions, including Wimbledon, the U.S. Open, and the Australian Open. She is handling her success well. Since she turned professional, she has played tennis all over the world and has earned millions of dollars.

Complete the interview about Serena Williams, using the present perfect or the present perfect continuous. Use the present perfect continuous only if the action is continuous or unfinished. Then answer the questions with information from Exercise D.

1. How long / she / play tennis?

   Q: _____?

   A: _____.

2. How long / she / live in California?

   Q: _____?

   A: _____.

3. she / win any competitions / since her first tournament?

   Q: _____?

   A: _____.

4. How much money / she / earn / since she began her career?

   Q: _____?

   A: _____.

Read the clues and complete the crossword puzzle.

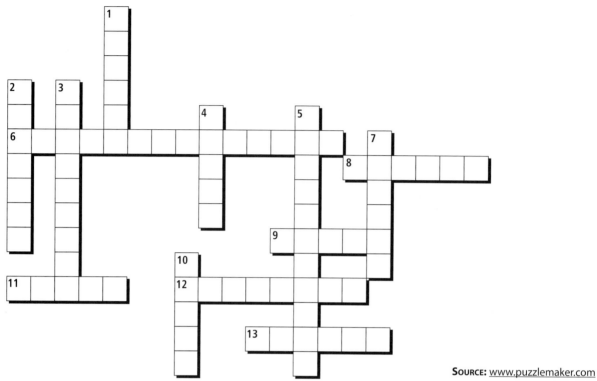

SOURCE: www.puzzlemaker.com

Across

6. movies that usually take place in the future

8. very scary film

9. very strange

11. another word for *hilarious*

12. about love

13. not interesting

Down

1. movie with a lot of fighting and killing

2. movie with singing and dancing

3. hand-drawn or computer-generated characters and scenery

4. not serious; almost stupid

5. movie about real-life events

7. movie that makes you laugh

10. serious movie, not funny

Fill in the answers.

1. When you really feel like doing something, you are in the ◯__ __ __.

2. Another name for the TV is the ◯__ __◯.

3. If something is hilarious, it's very __ __◯◯__.

4. When you're stuck in ◯__ __ __ __◯__, you're usually late.

5. The place where you go to see a movie is called the ◯__◯__ __ __◯.

6. An old movie is sometimes called a __ __◯__ __ __ __.

7. Another word for a type of movie is a __◯◯__ __.

Now unscramble the circled letters. What's the new word? _____

Answer: entertainment

UNIT

Staying at Hotels

TOPIC PREVIEW

1 Look at the hotel bill. Then answer the questions.

Mr. Philip Paul		ROOM	1631
11 Rue Ravignan		ARRIVAL	09/14
Place Emil Goudeau		DEPARTURE	09/16
75018 Paris, France		TIME	15:52
CLUB ONE MEMBER # PP2139			

NOVA HOTEL

DATE	REFERENCE	DESCRIPTION	AMOUNT
9/14	13:13	Local Call	Free (Club One member)
9/14	08:32	Overseas Call	40.34
9/14	3036	Internet access	Free (Club One member)
9/14	2765	Laundry	36.00
9/14		Room 1631	179.00
9/14	3036	Internet access	Free (Club One member)
9/14	2762	Room Service	18.92
9/15	2762	Room Service	26.45
9/15	09:52	Local Call	Free (Club One member)
9/15	428	Photocopies	Free (Club One member)
9/15	3036	Internet access	Free (Club One member)
9/15	758	Local Fax	Free (Club One member)
9/15		Room 1631	179.00
9/15	09562	Airport Shuttle	30.00
		BALANCE	509.71
		VAT 7.00%	35.68
		TOTAL INCLUDING VAT	545.39

1. What date did Mr. Paul check in? _____

2. How much did he pay for phone calls, faxes, and Internet usage? _____

3. What other hotel services did he use? _____

4. How much is the tax? _____

2 What hotel services were most important to Mr. Paul? Circle the hotel services he used more than once. Underline the services he did not use at all.

Internet access   telephone   airport shuttle   minibar

wake-up service   laundry   room service

3 WHAT ABOUT YOU? Which hotel services are important to you? Complete the paragraph.

> The most important hotel service for me is _____ because
> _____. Of course, _____ is also an important
> service, but _____ is not important to me at all. I can live without it!

Read the Nova Hotel's Club One brochure. Then read the statements and check true or false.

CLUB ONE

Club One is our special member program available to you. You don't have to pay a fee to join Club One. It's free! As a Club One member, just pick up your key at the desk, and your room is prepared exactly as you wish. We'll have a welcome beverage and snack waiting for you there at no charge. And you'll recieve a 10% discount on all room service orders. We offer many other member specials, including free local phone calls, free fax, free copies, and free high-speed Internet access. Become a member today!

	true	false
1. You have to pay to join Club One.	☐	☐
2. Club One members get some free food and drinks in their rooms.	☐	☐
3. Room service is free for Club One members.	☐	☐
4. Internet access is not free for Club One members.	☐	☐
5. Club One members can make local phone calls for free.	☐	☐

LESSON 1

Put the conversation in order. Write the number on the line.

_1_ Can I speak with Kevin Mercer, please? He's staying in room 376.

____ That's right.

____ Yes. Could you tell him Barbara called? Please ask him to call me back at 31–56–97.

____ One moment, please . . . I'm sorry. There's no answer. Can I take a message?

____ Barbara at 31–56–97?

____ Is that all?

_7_ Yes, that's it. Thank you very much.

6 **Choose the best response. Circle the letter.**

1. "Is Rosa Mayall in?"
   a. Too bad.　　**b.** I'd love to.　　**c.** Yes, just a moment please.

2. "When will she be back?"
   a. In an hour.　　**b.** Yesterday.　　**c.** Tell her I called.

3. "Can I leave her a message?"
   a. Not yet.　　**b.** Sure.　　**c.** No, thanks. I'll call back later.

7 **The fortune-teller is predicting the future. Read her predictions. Then rewrite the sentences, using <u>will</u>.**

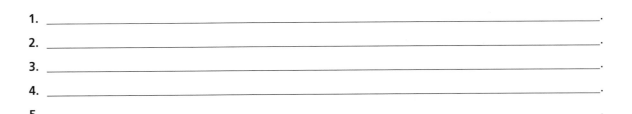

3. When you are in Barcelona, you meet an old friend.

2. Then, you're taking a trip to Barcelona.

4. Your friend is going to offer you an exciting job in Spain.

1. Next week, you are going to win a prize.

5. Next month, you are moving to Spain!

1. _____ .

2. _____ .

3. _____ .

4. _____ .

5. _____ .

FACTOID: TELEPHONES

There are more than 600 million telephone lines today, yet almost half the world's population has never made a phone call.

Source: www.didyouknow.cd

8 ▷ **Read the phone conversation. Then complete the message sheet.**

A: Hello. I'd like to speak with Ms. Marina Santiago, please.

B: One moment, please. I'll ring Ms. Santiago's room . . . I'm sorry, but there's no answer. Would you like to call back later?

A: No, I'd like to leave a message. Please tell her that Anna Streed called. I'll be at 555–8723 until 5:00 today.

B: OK, Ms. Anna Street . . .

A: No, it's Streed, S-T-R-E-E-D— that's D as in "door."

B: Oh, OK, Ms. Anna Streed, 555–8723. I'll make sure she gets the message.

A: Thank you.

To <u>Marina Santiago</u>

Date _____9/14_____ Time _____3:15_____ A.M. ☐ P.M. ☒

WHILE YOU WERE OUT

☐ Mr./ ☐ Ms./ ☐ Mrs. _____

Phone _____
　　　　Area code　　　Number　　　Extension

☐ telephoned　　　　☐ please call
☐ returned your call　☐ will call back

Message: _____
_____

LESSON 2

9 ▷ **Complete the conversation. Write the letter on the line.**

A: Hello. I'm checking in. The name is Chang, Ken Chang.

B: ____
　　1.

A: Actually, I don't need a suite. It's just me, so a single room will be fine.

B: ____
　　2.

A: Smoking, please. Does the room have Internet access?

B: ____
　　3.

A: That's great. Thanks.

B: ____
　　4.

A: Here's my credit card.

B: ____
　　5.

a. No problem. Would you like a smoking or non-smoking room?

b. Thank you.

c. Yes, sir. That's a suite with a king-size bed, right?

d. You're welcome. And how do you want to pay?

e. Yes, all the rooms in the hotel have free wireless Internet access.

1. Mr. and Mrs. Benson, traveling alone:

a single room with a king-size bed

2. Jon and Marie Smith with their two young children:

_____

3. Mrs. Wu, with her husband, her two sons, and her mother:

_____

4. Laura Cole, planning to have meetings in her hotel room:

_____

5. Nicole Maxwell and her five-year-old daughter:

_____

6. Julio Chavez, traveling alone on business:

_____

 Look at the pictures and complete the sentences with <u>'d better</u> or <u>'d better not</u>.

1. Hey, look at that sign. We _____

_____ .

2. Blackbird is a very popular restaurant.

You _____

_____ .

3. It's after midnight. We _____

_____ .

4. The movie starts in three minutes.

You _____

_____ .

LESSON 3

12 ▸ **Label the pictures.**

1. _____

2. _____

3. _____

4. _____

5. _____

13 ▸ **Look at the pictures. Then complete the conversations.**

1. **A:** Guest services. May I help you?

   B: Yes, please. Could you bring up some

   _____?

   A: Certainly.

   B: And I could use a _____, too.
   My hair is wet, and I don't see one in the bathroom.

   A: Sure. We'll bring those up right away.
   Anything else?

   B: Oh, yes. I have a lot of dirty clothes. Could

   someone please _____?

   A: Yes, of course.

   B: I think that's all. Thanks!

2. **A:** Front Desk. May I help you?

   B: Yes, I'd like to go for a swim. Is the

   _____ still open?

   A: No, I'm sorry, it closed at 9:00.

   B: Oh. Well, maybe a workout. How about the

   _____?

   A: No, it also just closed.

   B: Oh, no. Well, I guess I'll have to do some work then.

   Is the _____ still open?

   A: No, I'm sorry, it closed at 6:30. But you do
   have high-speed Internet access in your room.

   B: Oh, OK. Thanks.

LESSON 4

 Read the online articles. Then answer the questions below, according to the information in the articles.

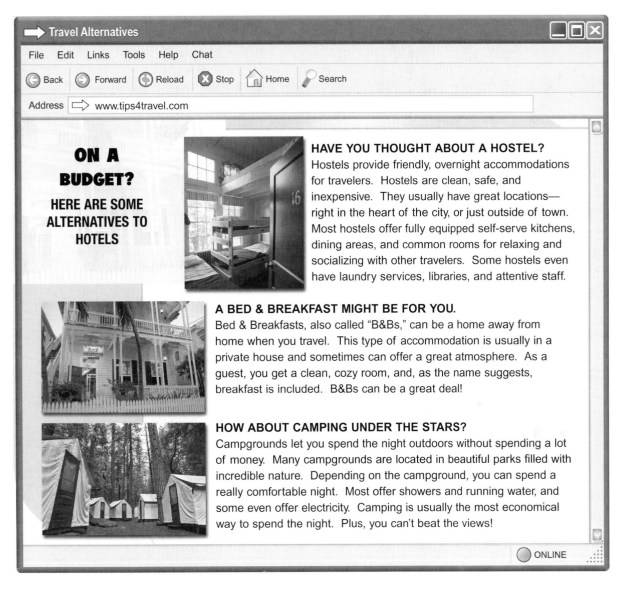

ON A BUDGET?

HERE ARE SOME ALTERNATIVES TO HOTELS

HAVE YOU THOUGHT ABOUT A HOSTEL?
Hostels provide friendly, overnight accommodations for travelers. Hostels are clean, safe, and inexpensive. They usually have great locations—right in the heart of the city, or just outside of town. Most hostels offer fully equipped self-serve kitchens, dining areas, and common rooms for relaxing and socializing with other travelers. Some hostels even have laundry services, libraries, and attentive staff.

A BED & BREAKFAST MIGHT BE FOR YOU.
Bed & Breakfasts, also called "B&Bs," can be a home away from home when you travel. This type of accommodation is usually in a private house and sometimes can offer a great atmosphere. As a guest, you get a clean, cozy room, and, as the name suggests, breakfast is included. B&Bs can be a great deal!

HOW ABOUT CAMPING UNDER THE STARS?
Campgrounds let you spend the night outdoors without spending a lot of money. Many campgrounds are located in beautiful parks filled with incredible nature. Depending on the campground, you can spend a really comfortable night. Most offer showers and running water, and some even offer electricity. Camping is usually the most economical way to spend the night. Plus, you can't beat the views!

ONLINE

1. Which is usually the cheapest type of accommodation? _____

2. Which type of accommodation has a kitchen? _____

3. Where can you always get breakfast? _____

4. Where can you probably use your computer? _____

5. Where might you be able to wash clothes? _____

6. Where should you stay if you like to meet new people? _____

7. Which type of accommodation is best for you if you like hiking and fishing?

_____

CHALLENGE. **Read the statements. Which accommodation is best for each of these people, based on the online articles in Exercise 14? Give advice, using had better (not) or should (not).**

> I'm a student, and I like to meet new and interesting people when I travel.

1. He should _____

_____.

> Peter always wants to save money, but on vacation, I like a comfortable bed and some privacy.

2. They _____

_____.

> Location is everything to me. I've got to be close to the clubs and shops.

3. _____

_____.

> I'd rather spend my vacation in the countryside than sightseeing in the city. Comfort's not so important to me.

4. _____

_____.

 WHAT ABOUT YOU? Which type of accommodation is best for you? Why? Complete the paragraph.

I would like to stay

A Complete the sentences, using <u>will</u> or <u>won't</u>.
Use contractions when possible.

A: _____ you be staying with us another night?
1.

B: No, we _____. But I think we _____ be back
2.   3.

next month.

A: Great. How _____ you be paying today?
4.

B: I _____ use my credit card, if that's OK.
5.

A: Sure. That _____ be fine.
6.

B Look at the pictures. What do you think the man is going to do?
Write sentences with a form of <u>be going to</u> or <u>not be going to</u>.

1. _____   2. _____   3. _____

_____   _____   _____

4. _____   5. _____

_____   _____

Complete the sentences. Use the correct form of <u>be going to</u> if there is a plan for the future or <u>will</u> if there is not a plan.

1. **A:** What are you doing this weekend?

   B: I _____ a play. How about you?
   _{see}

   A: No plans. Maybe I _____ to the movies.
   _{go}

2. **A:** Have you decided about your vacation yet?

   B: Yes, we have. We _____ to India!
   _{go}

   A: Wow! When _____ you _____?
   _{leave}

   B: We _____ out on the 20th.
   _{fly}

   A: That's fantastic. Where _____ you _____?
   _{stay}

   B: We _____.
   _{camp}

3. **A:** Guess what? I _____ into a new apartment next week.
   _{move}

   B: That's great news! I _____ you on moving day if you like.
   _{help}

   A: Thanks! It's this Saturday at 9 A.M. OK?

   B: Oh, no! I _____ my sister at the airport then.
   _{pick up}

   A: No problem. Just come by when you're free.

D **Complete the sentences. Circle the best answers.**

1. I went to the office early because I (had better / had to) finish some work.

2. You (must not / don't have to) tell Linda about the surprise party. It's a secret.

3. You have a lot of homework. You really (ought to / could) get started.

4. We (were supposed to / had better) be at the airport by now! I hope we don't miss our plane!

5. I don't think this restaurant accepts credit cards. (Could / Must) we pay by check?

JUST FOR FUN

1 WORD FIND. Look at the pictures. The words are across (→), down (↓), diagonal (↘), and sometimes backwards (←). Circle the six hotel services. Then write the hotel services on the lines.

```
O  R  C  N  Q  Y  Z  B  S  S  N  B
B  R  A  T  L  L  F  H  T  Y  O  E
B  A  O  B  S  A  O  X  F  H  Z  L
G  Y  B  B  I  E  A  G  R  Q  Y  L
R  B  U  Y  S  N  V  J  G  N  W  S
S  B  C  H  S  R  I  B  A  F  L  E
S  G  I  J  W  I  X  M  T  U  S  R
C  N  Y  E  H  S  T  L  X  O  U  V
E  Y  Q  Y  C  T  X  D  Q  Z  I
R  O  O  M  S  E  R  V  I  C  E  C
Y  R  D  N  U  A  L  C  I  N  Z  E
P  R  M  E  O  X  O  X  Y  U  G  U
```

Source: Created by Puzzlemaker at DiscoverySchool.com

_____   _____

_____   _____

_____   _____

2 TAKE A GUESS! Which of these hotels actually exists? After you guess, read the information at the bottom of the page.

Source: www.jul.com

Answer to Exercise 2: It's the third one. "Jules' Undersea Lodge" in Key Largo, Florida is the world's only underwater hotel. Guests must scuba dive 21 feet, or 6.5 meters, beneath the surface of the sea to check in! The staff of Jules' Undersea Lodge remains on duty 24 hours a day to provide whatever services the guests may need.

UNIT 4

Cars and Driving

TOPIC PREVIEW

 Read the conversation. Then complete the rental request.

AGENT: Hi. How can I help you?

RENTER: Hello. I'd like to make a reservation for June 20th.

AGENT: Certainly. Let's see . . . There's a Fiat Siena available.

RENTER: Is it air-conditioned?

AGENT: No, I'm sorry, it isn't. I have a Renault Clio that is.

RENTER: That'll be great.

AGENT: How long do you need the car for?

RENTER: For eight days.

AGENT: No problem. You can pick the car up in the afternoon at L & M Car Rental's main office downtown.

RENTER: And do I drop it off there, too?

AGENT: No, you have to drop it off at the airport, no later than 3 P.M.

RENTER: OK, that's fine.

AGENT: Can you please fill this out . . .

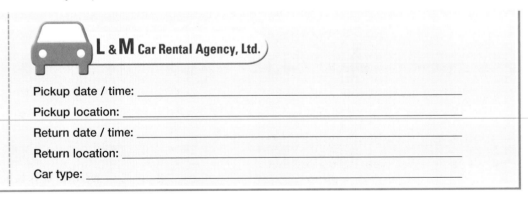

L & M Car Rental Agency, Ltd.

Pickup date / time: _____

Pickup location: _____

Return date / time: _____

Return location: _____

Car type: _____

 Choose the correct response. Circle the letter.

1. "How can I help you?"

   a. No, thanks.　　　b. I have a reservation.　　　c. Certainly, sir.

2. "Do you need an automatic transmission or manual?"

   a. That's correct.　　　b. Oh, yes.　　　c. Either way.

3. "Can I see your driver's license?"

   a. Here you go.　　　b. No, I don't.　　　c. Here are the keys.

4. "Is that OK?"

   a. Good morning.　　　b. That'll be fine.　　　c. I have a reservation.

LESSON 1

3 **Label the car parts.**

1. <u>d a s h b o a r d</u>

2. _ _ _ _ _ _ _ _ _ _ _ _ _ _ _ _

3. _ _ _ _ _ _ _ _ _ _ _ _ _ _ _

4. _ _ _ _ _

5. _ _ _ _ _ _ _ _ _ _ _ _

6. _ _ _ _ _ _ _ _ _ _ _ _

_ _ _ _ _

7. _ _ _ _ _ _ _ _ _ _

8. _ _ _ _ _ _ _ _ _ _

9. _ _ _ _ _ _ _ _ _ _ _

10. _ _ _ _ _ _

4 **Choose the correct response. Write the letter on the line.**

1. "I had an accident today." ____

2. "Are you OK?" ____

3. "How did it happen?" ____

4. "Luckily, I was wearing my seat belt." ____

5. "Was there much damage?" ____

a. The other driver was speeding.

b. Not really. The other driver will have to replace a taillight.

c. Thank goodness.

d. Yes, I'm OK. No one was hurt.

e. How awful.

• FACTOID •

WHY DO PEOPLE RENT CARS?

Most cars rented are rented for vacations (66%). About one in five (21%) cars are rented for business reasons. One-tenth (10%) are rented for a combination of business and pleasure travel.

SOURCE: www.traveldailynews.com

5 ▶ **Complete the conversation. Use the simple past tense or the past continuous.**

A: Hi Sandra. What's wrong?

B: I _____ an accident on the way home today.
　　　　 1. have

A: Oh, no! How _____ it _____?
　　　　　　　　　　　　　　　　　　　2. happen

B: Well, I _____ home when my sister
　　　　　　3. drive

　　 _____. She _____ what I
　　　4. call　　　　　　**5. ask**

　　 _____, and I _____ her
　　　6. do　　　　　　**7. tell**

　　 I _____ home and would see her soon.
　　　　8. go

　　 But she _____ she had a funny story that
　　　　　　　　9. say

　　 she just <u>had</u> to tell me. Anyway, by the end of the story, I _____ so hard
　　　　　　　　　　　　　　　　　　　　　　　　　　　　　　　10. laugh

　　 I couldn't see—and I _____ right into a stop sign.
　　　　　　　　　　　　11. drive

6 ▶ **WHAT ABOUT YOU? Have you or has someone you know ever had an accident? What happened? Write a note to a friend about it.**

LESSON 2

7 ▶ **Look at the pictures. Write the letter of the correct picture after each phrasal verb.**

1. fill up ____ 　 **2.** turn on ____ 　 **3.** drop off ____ 　 **4.** turn off ____ 　 **5.** pick up ___

8 CHALLENGE. **Complete the note below. Use the correct phrasal verb from Exercise 7. Sometimes you will need to use direct object pronouns.**

Hi, Lisa!

I made an appointment to have Stan fix the car today. Can you _____ at the

service station this afternoon? Tell Stan that the left turn signal isn't working. This morning I could

_____ , but now it's stuck, and I can't seem to _____ .

Ask him to call me when the car is done. I'll _____ on my way home from work.

Love, Daniel

P.S. While you're there, could you _____ the tank? See you tonight!

9 **Choose the correct response. Circle the letter.**

1. "It'll be $9.00 to dry-clean this dress."

   a. OK. When can I pick it up?   **b.** Fill it up, please.   **c.** How about noon?

2. "Fill it up with regular, please."

   a. Sure. I'll see you at 10:00.   **b.** Yes, that's all.   **c.** Yes, ma'am. Anything else?

3. "Your computer is working. But it looks like the printer won't turn on."

   a. Yes, sir.   **b.** Can you fix it?   **c.** Terrific! I'll see you then.

4. "The seat belt on the passenger side is stuck. Can you take a look for me?"

   a. No, thanks.   **b.** That's great!   **c.** Sure. Can you drop off the car at 3:00?

LESSON 3

10 **Choose the best answer from the box to complete each sentence. Use each phrase only once.**

a convertible   a van   an SUV   a luxury car   a compact car

1. Mrs. Jeter drives _____ to take her husband to work and their
   five children to school every morning.

2. If you just need a car that's small and easy to park, _____ would
   be great for you.

3. Mavis loves hiking. She has _____ with four-wheel drive that she
   can drive on rough roads when she takes a trip to the mountains.

4. Peter thinks that owning _____ is really cool. He said, "You can have
   the roof down and enjoy the sun, wind, and beautiful sky when the weather is nice."

5. Jack is the president of a big company and he drives _____ with
   expensive leather seats.

11 Read the ads for three cars. Then choose the best answer to each question, according to the ads. Circle the letter.

The Ramuno is really inexpensive, and you'll find it easier than ever to own one today. You can start saving money because it's good on gas. You can even save time parking when you drive a Ramuno—with the Ramuno's size, you'll never have to worry if you can only find a tight parking spot.

RAMUNO

Love outdoor adventures? Feel the power of the four-wheel drive Vicic. It'll take you just about anywhere. The new design allows you to enjoy a comfortable ride even on the toughest mountain roads. Come test-drive it today!

VICIC

Zatec You'll be amazed by how the Zatec provides comfortable seating for nine people and still has plenty of cargo room. Whether it's a few suitcases for your family's road trip or all the bags from a long day's shopping at the mall, you won't have any problem fitting them all in.

1. Which of the three cars can take the most passengers?

    a. the Vicic   **b.** the Zatec   **c.** the Ramuno

2. What do you think the Zatec is?

    a. a sports car   **b.** a full-size car   **c.** a van

3. Which of the three cars is most likely a compact car?

    a. the Ramuno   **b.** the Vicic   **c.** the Zatec

12 CHALLENGE. **Which of the three cars is best for each person? Give suggestions, based on the information in the ads in Exercise 11. Explain your reasons.**

1. Bryan is planning a cross-country road trip with his girlfriend. They want to do a lot of sightseeing in the countryside and go hiking in the mountains.

    _____

2. Rachel's got four kids, and she works part time. She has a lot of driving to do between work, the kids, and shopping. And she needs to carry a lot of things around.

    _____

3. Danny recently graduated from college and has just started working. He doesn't have a lot of money. He's single and lives by himself. His office is on a busy street downtown, far away from where he lives. He plans to drive to work.

    _____

 13 WHAT ABOUT YOU? **Have you ever rented a car? If not, would you like to? What kind of car would you like to rent, and why?**

LESSON 4

 Read the rental car safety tips and the information about driving in Luxembourg.

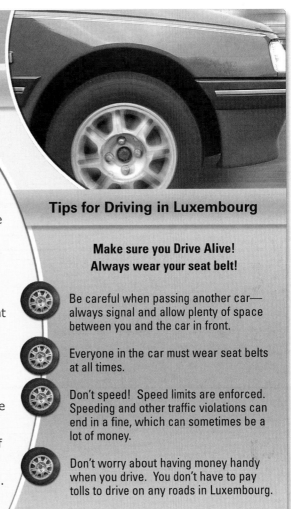

RENTING A CAR?

Safety Tips for a Safe Drive

Driving an unfamiliar car in an unfamiliar city can be stressful and dangerous. But if you follow these tips, you'll be fine. Before you leave the rental car lot, be sure you know how to work the headlights and how to turn on and off all the signals and the interior light. Make sure everything is working properly. You should check the windshield wipers to make sure they work, too. Adjust the seat and mirrors so that you are comfortable and can see other cars around you on the road. Check the seat belts: Is there one for every passenger? Are they easy to use? And finally, if you like to listen to the radio as you drive, tune in a local station that meets your tastes. You avoid a lot of accidents, and a lot of stress, if you take care of everything before you hit the road.

Tips for Driving in Luxembourg

**Make sure you Drive Alive!
Always wear your seat belt!**

Be careful when passing another car—always signal and allow plenty of space between you and the car in front.

Everyone in the car must wear seat belts at all times.

Don't speed! Speed limits are enforced. Speeding and other traffic violations can end in a fine, which can sometimes be a lot of money.

Don't worry about having money handy when you drive. You don't have to pay tolls to drive on any roads in Luxembourg.

Source: www.driving.drive-alive.co.uk
Image: budgetstockphoto.com

Complete each sentence. Circle the letter.

1. Driving a rental car can be stressful because _____.

   a. the car is dangerous   b. it's not your car   c. you don't speak the language

2. You should check the seat belts _____.

   a. before you leave the rental car lot   b. before you get on the highway   c. while you're driving

3. In Luxembourg, seat belts must be worn _____.

   a. by the driver only   b. by children only   c. by everyone in the car

4. If you drive too fast in Luxembourg, you'll have to _____.

   a. talk to the police   b. pay a lot of money   c. leave the country

15 **WHAT ABOUT YOU?** **What helpful hints would you give someone driving in your country for the first time? Use the ideas below to write a "Drive Alive" website for your country.**

Tips for driving in _____

Make sure you Drive Alive! Always _____!

Traffic laws: _____
_____

Customs: _____
_____

Local driving habits: _____
_____

Other: _____
_____

○ ONLINE

GRAMMAR BOOSTER

A **Complete each sentence, using the simple past tense or the past continuous.**

1. They were having dinner when _____.

2. While _____, it started to rain.

3. While Marie was watching TV, her husband _____.

4. When _____, I was leaving my office.

5. He had an accident while _____.

B **Rewrite the sentences in reported speech.**

1. He said, "I'm leaving early today."

   He said he was leaving early today _____.

2. She said, "I'm working really hard on the project."

   _____.

3. I told him, "We're eating dinner at 8:00."

   _____.

4. They said, "It's raining outside."

   _____.

5. He told her, "They're studying at the library this evening."

   _____.

C Look at the pictures. Write a story about what happened, using the words and phrases.

| drive |
| talk on cell phone |
| not pay attention |

| run in front of |
| stop |

| hit |
| hurt |
| damage |

(blank lined writing area)

D Put the words in order and write sentences. If a sentence can be written in two ways, write it both ways.

1. dropped / Margo / off / the car

   Margo dropped off the car. OR Margo dropped the car off .

2. up / it / Sam / picked

   _____ .

3. the tank / filled / I / up

   _____ .

4. can't / turn / on / Sue / the headlights

   _____ .

5. turn / off / I / can't / them

   _____ .

6. like / He'd / it / to / drop / off / at noon

   _____ .

7. I / to / need / up / it / fill

   _____ .

8. picked / the car / already / William / up / has

   _____ .

JUST FOR FUN

1 FIGURE IT OUT! **Figure out the riddles. Read the clue and write the car part.**

1. You turn this on to let other drivers know you are turning right or left.

☐ ☐ ☐ ☐ ☐
 　　4　　5

2. When it's raining, you turn these on.

☐ ☐ ☐ ☐ ☐ ☐ ☐ ☐　☐ ☐ ☐ ☐ ☐
 　　6　　　　　　　　　　　　　3

3. You press this down to make the car go faster.

☐ ☐ ☐　☐ ☐ ☐ ☐
 　7　　　　2

4. You look into this to see what is behind you.

☐ ☐ ☐ ☐ ☐ ☐ ☐　☐ ☐ ☐ ☐ ☐
 　　　8　　　　　　　　1

5. You push this in to move the gearshift in a manual transmission car.

☐ ☐ ☐ ☐ ☐
 9

What's the title?

☐ ☐ ☐ ☐　☐ ☐ ☐　☐ ☐ ☐ ☐ ☐ ☐
9 5 3 7　5 6 2　2 3 1 8 1 6 4

2 TAKE A GUESS! **Read these unusual driving rules and regulations. Check true or false. After you finish, check your answers.**

	true	false
1. Because the streets were so crowded, Julius Caesar made a law stating that chariots could not travel in Rome during the day.	☐	☐
2. In ancient times, if a driver in Athens was dirty or poorly dressed, the police could refuse to let that person drive.	☐	☐
3. Most European countries drive on the right because when Napoleon entered these countries, he said they had to drive vehicles the same way that the French did.	☐	☐
4. You must drive on the right through the English Channel Tunnel (also known as the Eurotunnel or Chunnel).	☐	☐

Answers to Exercise 2: All of the statements are true except the last one. You don't drive in the Eurotunnel. When you arrive at the terminal, you park your car on a train wagon, and the train takes you across. When you get off the train at the other end, you get your car and then you have to choose the correct side of the road to drive on—right in France, left in England.

Personal Care and Appearance

TOPIC PREVIEW

1 Complete each conversation. Choose the correct response. Circle the letter.

> I have to pick up something for my wife's birthday later. Feel like helping me?

> a. I'll just go myself.
>
> b. Sure. No problem.

①

> I'm nervous about making the presentation at the meeting tomorrow.

> a. Don't worry. You'll be fine.
>
> b. Wish me luck.

②

> I have to get to the office. I'm expecting an important call at three.

> a. OK. See you back at the office.
>
> b. I don't have much time today.

③

> I'm going out for dinner later. Want to come with me?

> a. It'll be a piece of cake.
>
> b. I'm sorry. I think I'll pass.

④

2 Read these people's statements. Think of at least two products each person might buy at a drugstore. Write the names of the products on their shopping bags.

1. _____

"The dentist said I needed to take better care of my teeth."

2. _____

"I just got back from the salon. I really want to try out some of the products they use there!"

3. _____

"I feel terrible! I'd better get something for this cold."

3 WHAT ABOUT YOU? What type of products do you usually buy? Rank the categories from 1 to 4 (1 = buy often, 2 = buy sometimes, 3 = don't buy often, 4 = almost never buy). Then use the prompts to complete the paragraph about your favorite product.

____ Hair care   ____ Tooth care   ____ Skin care   ____ Shaving   ____ Makeup

My favorite _____ product is _____.
           (hair care / tooth care / skin care / shaving / makeup)

I buy it at _____ about _____. I especially
              (name of store)   (how often?)

like _____ because _____
        (brand)

_____.

LESSON 1

4 Look at the responses. Write the questions or statements to complete the conversation.

A: _____?
                                              1.

B: Nail clippers? Did you look in aisle three?

A: _____.
                                              2.

B: I'm sorry. Let me have a look in the back. . . . I'm sorry. We're out of them.

A: _____?
                                              3.

B: Yes, the nail files should be right over here. Here you go.

A: _____.
                                              4.

B: You're very welcome.

5 Complete the sentences. Circle the correct words.

1. This store doesn't have (much / many) combs.

2. I can't find (some / any) sunscreen, but here's (some / any) body lotion.

3. Do you have (much / a lot of) razor blades at home?

4. She doesn't have (much / many) hair spray left.

5. Emma needs (some / any) dental floss.

6. Helen doesn't need (some / much) soap.

7. Do you have (any / many) shaving cream?

8. I have (some / any) extra shampoo.

9. I found a razor, but there aren't (some / any) razor blades here.

6 Complete the word webs. Write products or categories on the lines.

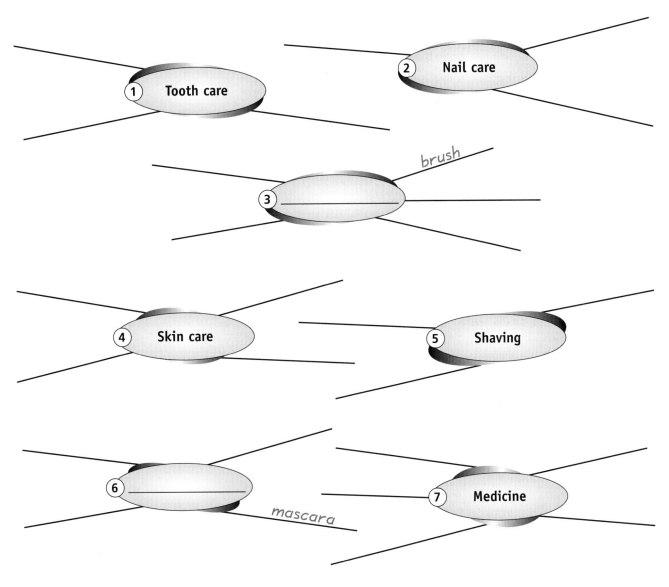

LESSON 2

 7 Complete the conversation. Write the letter on the line.

A: I have an appointment for a facial with Paula.

B: _____
   1.

A: Can I get a manicure in the meantime?

B: _____
   2.

A: No, thanks. Actually, I'd love a cup of tea.

B: _____
   3.

A: Thanks. How long will I have to wait?

B: _____
   4.

a. Yes, but someone's ahead of you. Can I get you some coffee?

b. Not long. Just a few minutes.

c. I'm sorry. She's running a little late.

d. Certainly. . . . Here you go.

8 ▷ **Fill in the answers.**

1. My hair is dirty. I need a __ __ __ __ __ (__) __ .

2. Your fingernails look great. When did you get your __ __ (__) __ __ __ __ __ ?

3. His hair was too long, so he got a __ (__) __ __ __ __ __ .

4. I don't care for that beard on you. You should go to the barber and get a (__) __ __ __ __ .

5. Do you have a different color nail __ __ (__) __ __ __ ? I'd prefer pink.

Now unscramble the circled letters. What's the new word? _____

9 ▷ **Complete each sentence with <u>someone</u> or <u>anyone</u>.**

1. I know _____ who works at the salon downtown.

2. Can _____ help me?

3. I'm sorry. We don't have _____ available to help you now.

4. There's _____ ahead of you. Can you wait?

5. Did you meet _____ interesting at the hair salon?

6. There isn't _____ waiting for you at the reception desk.

LESSON 3

10 ▷ **Choose the correct response. Circle the letter.**

1. "How long will I have to wait?"

   a. This is our slow day.   b. I don't think so.   c. About twenty minutes.

2. "Can I charge it to my room?"

   a. Cash or credit?   b. Sure. No problem.   c. Ten percent.

3. "Would it be possible to get a pedicure, too?"

   a. I think so. Let me check.   b. How can I help you?   c. I guess I'll wait.

4. "How much do you charge for a haircut?"

   a. Yes, you can charge it.   b. Short hair is €35, and €45 for long hair.   c. About thirty-five minutes.

5. "Can I possibly get a shave and a haircut? I don't have an appointment."

   a. I don't mind waiting.   b. I think I'll pass.   c. I'm sorry. We're fully booked.

6. "Is it customary to leave a tip for a massage?"

   a. Yes, about 15 percent of the total.   b. That'll be fine.   c. She can see you in ten minutes.

11 Look at the pictures. Check all the sentences that are true, according to the pictures.

1. ☐ **a.** Rosa is going into the salon.
   ☐ **b.** Rosa has an appointment.
   ☐ **c.** Rosa has to cancel her appointment.

2. ☐ **a.** Rosa is late for her appointment.
   ☐ **b.** The salon isn't very busy.
   ☐ **c.** Rosa will have to wait.

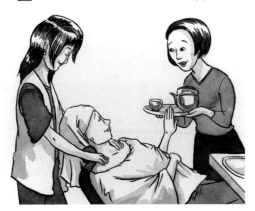

3. ☐ **a.** Rosa is leaving the salon.
   ☐ **b.** Rosa is getting a massage.
   ☐ **c.** Rosa doesn't want anything to drink.

4. ☐ **a.** Rosa didn't get a haircut.
   ☐ **b.** Rosa is pleased with her haircut.
   ☐ **c.** Rosa just got a pedicure.

12 Write a short paragraph about Rosa's day at the salon.

13 WHAT ABOUT YOU? How do you like to pamper yourself?

_____ go to the hair salon   _____ go shopping

_____ get a pedicure   _____ get a massage

_____ get a shave and a haircut   _____ other: _____

LESSON 4

 14 Read the online article. Then read the statements and check <u>true</u> or <u>false</u>.

→ **Cosmetic Surgery Vacations** ⬜🔲✕

Cosmetic surgery vacations are the latest trend in cosmetic surgery. These holidays can take you to foreign lands, sometimes save you money, and offer you privacy.

But be careful—all surgery is serious. Here are some of the reasons for a cosmetic surgery vacation—and some important things to keep in mind.

Cosmetic Surgery Vacations

PRIVACY

Cosmetic vacations are great if you want to keep your surgery private. You don't have to tell anyone where you're going, or why. When you return home, friends and family will think you look great because you've just had a relaxing vacation.

SAVING MONEY

Many cosmetic surgery vacations take you to countries where costs for surgery can be relatively inexpensive. But in many places, surgery prices can be high for foreigners. So be sure to check before you go.

QUALIFIED DOCTORS

There are excellent surgeons throughout the world, but if you decide on a cosmetic holiday, be sure to ask a lot of questions. Here are some things to think about. Find out the qualifications of your doctor. Where did he or she study? Where has he or she worked? Ask how long he or she has been a doctor. Also, if possible, speak to past patients. Were they happy with their new appearance?

The above research is very important. After all, you will be placing your life in the surgeon's hands.

	true	false
1. Not all surgery is serious.	⬜	⬜
2. Cosmetic surgery vacations don't always save you money.	⬜	⬜
3. You should always do research on the doctor.	⬜	⬜
4. It is hard to find good surgeons around the world.	⬜	⬜

15 CHALLENGE. **Now answer the questions, according to the article.**

1. What are the reasons to choose a cosmetic surgery vacation?

_____

2. What are some things that are important in a doctor?

_____

3. Why do you think some people prefer not to tell anyone when they get cosmetic surgery?

_____

_____

16 WHAT ABOUT YOU? **Have you ever taken, or would you ever take, a cosmetic surgery vacation? Why or why not?**

A Look in the medicine cabinet. Write sentences, using words from the box.

tube	bottle	container	package	bar

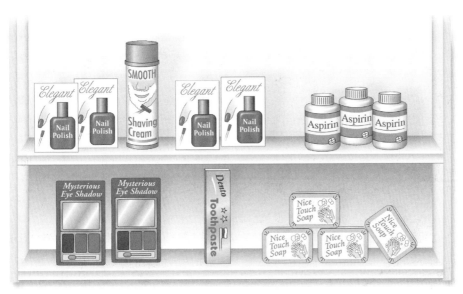

1. *There are four bottles of nail polish* .

2. _____ .

3. _____ .

4. _____ .

5. _____ .

6. _____ .

B Check the correct sentences.

1. ☐ **a.** There isn't enough soap.

   ☐ **b.** There isn't too many soap.

2. ☐ **a.** Do you have too much razors?

   ☐ **b.** Do you have too many razors?

3. ☐ **a.** I don't have too many makeup.

   ☐ **b.** I don't have enough makeup.

4. ☐ **a.** Does she have too many toothpaste?

   ☐ **b.** Does she have enough toothpaste?

5. ☐ **a.** There isn't too much shampoo.

   ☐ **b.** There isn't too many shampoo.

C Complete each sentence with <u>too much</u>, <u>too many</u>, or <u>enough</u>.

1. I couldn't wash my hair. There wasn't _____ shampoo left.

2. I'm going to the store. Do you have _____ flour to make the cake?

3. There are just _____ people here. I don't feel like waiting.

4. Don't you think that's _____ money for a pedicure? It's too expensive!

5. You bought _____ nail files. We only need one.

D Complete each sentence with <u>something</u> or <u>anything</u>.

1. We have _____ new at our salon.

2. He didn't take _____ for his headache.

3. Do you need _____ from the drugstore?

4. I didn't see _____ I like in the catalog.

5. I always buy _____ from that store.

6. I just can't relax. There is always _____ to do.

7. They gave me _____ to drink at the salon.

8. I don't know _____ about cosmetic surgery.

E Read the paragraph. Find five mistakes and correct them.

I went to the supermarket today because I needed to get nothing to cook

for my dinner party tonight. I wanted to buy some juice, too. But when I got

there, there wasn't nothing on the shelf! I went to the store manager and

told him that the shelves were empty. He apologized and said there was

anything wrong with the delivery truck. "It didn't come today," he told me.

He said I'd have to wait until the next day. Now I don't have something to

serve for the big party tonight. I've never seen nothing like this!

JUST FOR FUN

1 ▷ **WORD FIND. Find 15 personal care products in the puzzle. The words are across (→), down (↓), diagonal (↘), and sometimes backwards (←). Circle the items.**

R	A	Z	O	R	B	L	A	D	E	N	L	N	D	U
R	E	T	E	M	O	M	R	E	H	T	S	O	E	S
J	E	A	S	U	P	O	J	A	Q	H	T	I	O	T
F	G	P	T	U	Z	U	I	M	A	Z	H	T	D	Y
Q	F	B	P	A	N	R	E	V	J	S	V	O	O	Q
Y	L	S	R	I	S	S	I	K	U	T	P	L	R	T
Z	L	C	V	P	L	N	C	R	A	J	S	Y	A	H
E	Y	J	R	B	G	C	B	R	J	M	Z	D	N	S
O	V	A	H	C	S	H	L	T	E	W	G	O	T	U
C	Y	I	R	I	T	O	L	I	G	E	X	B	U	R
T	O	E	C	O	M	B	A	O	A	G	N	H	L	B
P	A	D	O	V	M	Y	A	P	U	N	C	W	J	R
M	P	T	W	W	Q	N	B	S	E	B	K	F	I	V
O	T	B	X	A	R	A	C	S	A	M	T	X	Q	F
A	W	R	U	S	Z	A	S	B	U	I	C	H	A	H

body lotion
brush
comb
deodorant
hair spray
makeup
mascara
nail clipper
razor
razor blade
shaving cream
soap
sunscreen
thermometer
toothbrush

SOURCE: Created by Puzzlemaker at <u>DiscoverySchool.com</u>

2 ▷ **TAKE A GUESS! Read these sentences about hair. Do you think they are true or false? Write T (true) or F (false) and then check your answers.**

1. ___ Hair grows about 12 millimeters per month and one hair lives for up to seven years.

2. ___ If you never cut your hair, it would grow to a length of 107 centimeters before falling out.

3. ___ There are 120,000 hairs on the average adult head.

4. ___ Hair grows faster in the summer, during sleep, and between the ages of 16 and 24.

5. ___ Between the ages of 40 and 50, women lose about 20 percent of their hair.

SOURCE: <u>www.ukhairdressers.com</u>

(BEFORE)   (AFTER)

Dr. M. J. Pilkington
COSMETIC SURGEON
CALL 1-800-NEWFACE

Answers to Exercise 2: All of the sentences are true.